DISCOVERING MODERN ART

Other Books by John P. Sedgwick, Jr.

Art Appreciation Made Simple
Structure and Evolution of the Major Cultures
Highlights: An Illustrated History of Art, with E. M. Upjohn

JOHN P. SEDGWICK, JR.

DISCOVERING MODERN ART

The intelligent layman's guide

to painting from Impressionism to Pop

RANDOM HOUSE New York

ACKNOWLEDGMENTS

Among the many people to whom I am indebted for ideas and assistance I would especially like to thank Bill Alexander and Bob Bernstein, who originally thought of such a book; Marian and the girls and all the Deelys for many a stimulating suggestion; Lou Ann Smith and Ruth Olson for consultation and advice; Fred Chappell for yeoman work on the manuscript; Ruth Latta and Ann Evans for timely pinch hitting; Joe Fox for patience, fortitude and labor beyond the call of duty; and Margaret Ann Harrell for a prodigy of rewriting and clarification almost beyond belief.

For My Parents

CONTENTS

LIST OF ILLUSTRATIONS

INTRODUCTION

In a poem in 1920 William Butler Yeats announced an age in which "Things fall apart; the centre cannot hold; Mere anarchy is loosed upon the world." For many people he could have been describing the scene of modern art, where things often seem to fall apart—fragmented, apparently unrecognizable, with no discernible purpose unless it be "mere anarchy." At times such an impression is not unwarranted, because it is perfectly true that practical jokes have been passed off as art. Nevertheless, whatever its appearance, modern art is not just imagination gone berserk. The best modern art is as serious and meaningful as most art forms of the past.

But because of its style, it is much more difficult to come to grips with. It seldom seeks to tell a story, and its symbols tend to be personal rather than public. While it has an unusual immediacy, it is also highly professional, even specialized, in its language. Partly for these reasons, partly because of its own inner nature, a modern work requires that the viewer have an "encounter" with it, and in doing so, bring as much of himself as he can.

No encounter is very promising unless both sides are serious and open themselves to a new experience. This the artist has emphatically done. As Harold Taylor * has written, "The conduct of the contemporary

* *Art and the Intellect*, New York, 1960, pp. 57–58.

artist is impeccable, he makes no claims except through his work, he threatens no one.

"The conduct of the observer, however, when he comes to the gallery or to the museum is a matter for the observer to determine for himself. If he screams with rage, if he feels himself threatened, insulted, or badgered, if he shouts that contemporary reality is not like that, if he cries for the Sistine Madonna, if he calls for the police, this reveals something in him, not in the artist or the art."

The leading spokesmen of modern art—not artists alone, but many writers, critics and dealers who for over a century have had to fight a hostile public—are for the most part quite serious, some to a degree of self-sacrifice that ought to be embarrassing to those skeptics who have drawn vast audiences or incomes out of questioning that sincerity. But the question of integrity is not the final issue: the fact that concerns us about modern art is that it won't go away.

While it won't go away, at the same time, like the mountain it will not necessarily come to us. We must go to it. The purpose of this book is to help point the way. Or rather, some of the various possible ways.

While the first purpose is to expose the reader to a variety of new kinds of art, and to the particular experience of a number of individual works, at the same time a point of view, even a line of argument, is inevitable.

Implicit in these pages is the concept that major art forms evolve in a given direction, and that in grasping the nature of this direction, one is better able to understand the meaning and value of any given work. One is better able to understand De Kooning having first known Matisse, and Matisse having first come to grips with the work of Cézanne. As the late anthropologist A.L. Kroeber insisted, "A true style does not travel so and so far and then retrace its steps; nor does it suddenly go off in a random new direction. The tendency is very strong for its direction not only to persevere up to a culmination, but to be irreversible."

For some time it has been my conviction that there is a central tradition in modern art, a tradition that has been insufficiently recognized, but once recognized, would help reveal the essential unity of a seeming chaos of forms and directions. For this reason I have occasionally felt impelled to indulge in an estimation or a prophecy about the directions most likely to prevail. The chief estimate is that the main line of artistic evolution for coming generations lies in the realm of what is most broadly known as abstract art. And a recurrent theme is that abstract art is not merely "abstracted," that it need by no means ignore profound issues and meaningful experiences.

The conclusion that abstract art—in its variable forms—will occupy a central position in future artistic development is based on several striking facts. Abstract painting is the favored heir of a long line of tendencies directly traceable to the musiclike effects developed by the sixteenth-century Venetians in the early use of oil on stretched canvas; and it goes even farther back, to tendencies important in Gothic and Romanesque art.

Secondly, this broad artistic approach called abstract offers at once the richest and most difficult arena in which the artist of our time may challenge himself. Finally, for all the momentary popularity of splinter movements, including "anti-art" groups, the most significant painting and sculpture being done today is still, even at this moment, to be found among abstract artists, young and old alike.

The history of art treats of the least useful and most expressive products of human industry . . .
—GEORGE KUBLER

A work of art is specific, local, individual; and it is our brightest token of universality . . .
—HENRI FOCILLON

DISCOVERING MODERN ART

I

WHY MODERN ART IS A PROBLEM

No one can explain how the notes of a Mozart melody, or the folds of a piece of Titian's drapery, produce their essential effects. If you do not feel it, no one by reasoning can make you feel it.
—JOHN RUSKIN

A poem should not mean
But be   —ARCHIBALD MACLEISH

Not long ago, it is said, a painting by a chimpanzee was slipped into an exhibition of abstract work. A well-known and distinguished museum curator had been asked to be one of the judges, and he paused a long time before this unidentified picture. "What did you think of that one?" asked a reporter later. "That," he answered, after some deliberation, "is one of the worst paintings by a chimpanzee that I've ever seen."

This story may not be true, but it could be, for paintings by chimpanzees can readily be distinguished, at least by the practiced eye, from good or even bad abstract paintings by humans. Not only that, but paintings by chimpanzees can be distinguished from paintings by orang-utans, just as the abstract paintings of children can be distinguished from those of adults, or the work of sane persons from the insane. Indeed, as the painter Odilon Redon insisted, "It is in the process of the subconscious that one must keep the greatest lucidity; without this, the art of painting would be like that of lunatics, children and fools."

But does the chimpanzee really paint the picture? In a demonstration in a zoo, paper and paint were given to two chimpanzees, who proceeded to throw the paint around in a rhythmic fashion. From time to time the person in charge would turn the paper sideways or upside down, and when he thought the picture done, would quickly withdraw it and substitute a fresh sheet. Which one was the monkey?

Because the untutored layman often feels that all modern paintings are pretty much indistinguishable, is he to conclude that the world of modern art is hopelessly obscure and that no one but a specialist can ever hope to find his way around? Not at all. It is partly a matter of familiarity with the style of the art, partly of familiarity with art language.

The electronics engineer, even the television repairman, has grown used to commanding a professional language that is on the whole incomprehensible to outsiders. Now, art is not like science; the two fields of activity are farther apart now than at any other time since the early Renaissance, when they were highly interchangeable. But art and science are alike in having become specialized, perhaps too much so —above all in their language. Scientists complain of the unnecessary jargon in their publications, and many artists and some art critics too despise the arbitrary inbred speech that has become all too habitual in art circles.

One sort of language—jargon and the use of special or recondite terms —is to be avoided. It is another kind of language that we seek to discover: the language of art. This means the way a work of art is put together, the way it "works"; it does not mean the technical knowledge of materials, processes, systems of rendering, etc. The layman can discover the most important aspects of the language of art simply through looking, with perhaps a little direction. In much the same way, the neophyte in music can get a great deal purely through listening, without necessarily reading music, playing an instrument or being acquainted with musical theory. But in art as in music, it does help to be directed toward certain things that are happening. Perhaps this last is the first job of the critic.

One way to introduce modern painting would be by analogy to an art form that is widely familiar today: the art of jazz.

Like jazz, abstract painting (Color Plate 5) is a searching art, one that *improvises* within a reigning rhythm and mood, and thus, makes itself. There is a new kind of freedom in both of these art forms, but in neither does the gain of freedom entail a loss of control or direction. What Bill Dixon said of jazz could be said of the best contemporary painting: ". . . there is no such thing as *complete* freedom. Freedom itself entails its own form of discipline, and if this were not the case, then the musician most qualified to play 'free' on a musical instrument would be a nonmusician, a person who does not know how to finger the instrument."

Another approach to modern painting is through finding a connection; that is, an association with something familiar. Children who have never seen a banjo have been heard to sing, "I come from Alabamy with a Band Aid on my knee." The words aren't what Stephen Foster meant, and they don't make all the sense in the world, but they do make at least momentary sense—something that can be handled.

Similarly, a great many people will seek and "find" images in abstract art which were certainly not intended by the artist and which probably cannot be attributed to a release of unconscious imagery. Making such a connection isn't necessarily harmful. It could be misleading in a final understanding of the work, but it could do positive service as a simple introduction to the work which might otherwise be inaccessible. Gratuitous images or interpretations will wear off with time; through exposure the more pertinent qualities will emerge.

That is, they will if the spectator is content to look and feel and does not insist upon "reading" or anticipating. In listening to music, one does not ordinarily expect to hear everyday sounds—fog horns, fire engines, children's cries or birds' songs. Yet many people cannot look at an abstract painting without expecting to "recognize" something. True, most people in the middle of the twentieth century are too sophisticated to ask a painting to tell a story (a demand that was widely made by the nineteenth-century public), but the layman (and alas, some contemporary critics) insist that a picture contain at least something they can identify.

Identify in what way? Let's take a table. But what is a table? To a small child it is something difficult to reach. If you ask a carpenter, it's a bunch of boards. To a housewife it presents a ceaseless challenge—now to load, now to clean. To a minister serving Communion it can have special associations and thus a symbolic value. To a scholar it may be a surface hidden somewhere beneath books and papers. To a poet it might be any of these—or a rhyme for "able."

So what is a table to the painter? The one thing he is not interested in is *the table as such*—and this applies just as much to the "realistic" old master as to the modern abstract artist. If a painter puts a table (or a reference to a table) in one of his pictures, it is because he is interested in some imaginative aspect or suggestive quality connected with it. This quality might reside in the new shapes and proportions discovered as the table is seen at different angles; it might be the surface as an arena in which to form an arrangement; it might depend upon the colors, textures or volumes that a given table projects in a given situation. Or it might emerge from the table as the instigator of human situations: something to put your elbows on, something hard to reach or the symbol of the groaning board. To the painter the table is not a reality in itself, but a bridge to a new reality which he envisions and creates.

The art of painting may encompass any visible thing. But insofar as painting is art, it is never content with the mere transcription of visual effects. Goethe warned that Art is called Art precisely because it is not

Nature. Painters, quite as much as poets, respond to an inner vision, and the whole history of art is more or less equally divided between representational (i.e., "realistic") and non-representational styles of portraying that vision.

This notion in no way precludes the artist's reference to nature. Already in a number of books there are photographs and diagrams which draw analogies between the forms and structures of modern abstract painting and natural phenomena such as weather-beaten trees, rock formations or patterns of stars. (Consider, among others, Gyorgy Kepes' *The New Landscape in Art and Science*.) Indeed, a most valuable function of art can lie in the artist's keener, more experienced and more unusual powers of vision. This is one whole facet of art—its ability to discover.

While art is not the antithesis of nature, neither is it content to take nature at face value. What art does is transform, redo, distill from nature something which is more truthful than what one ordinarily sees. As Sydney Harris put it in a newspaper column, "The 'real life' of a person is hidden both from the camera and from the tape-recorder—just as the 'real nature' of a table is hidden from the eye. We see only the appearance, the secondary characteristics . . . The primary task of art is to strip down the appearance, to remove the accidental, and to disclose the essential . . . [in *Hamlet*] Shakespeare took a 'true' Danish story and transformed it into a universal experience—not by saying 'This is how it was' but . . . 'This is what it means.' " All art deals in truths, but relatively few art forms (including literature) are primarily concerned with "realism." Valid realism in art is the attempt to get at further meanings by way of the objective observation of external phenomena. While this is a legitimate means, it hardly in itself constitutes art—whether in Dickens, Tolstoy and Hemingway, or Goya, Courbet and Toulouse-Lautrec.

What then is the *essence* of art? So far no one is known to have said.

This lack of definition does not mark a human inadequacy, but points instead to the indefinability of creative power. If art could be defined, there would be no such thing as art. For example, if it were definable, art would be reproducible, and if it could be effectively copied, it would no longer be that unique product of the human imagination which in its inmost nature must be considered either divine or ultimately mysterious.

If art cannot be defined, it can perhaps be qualified as a work of the imagination which has fought its way through earthly forms (words, sights or sounds) until they have been forged into an unprecedented vessel. The power of imagination in art lies not in idle speculation, but in the depth and poignancy with which it evokes the inner meanings of joy and pain, absurdity, struggle and aspiration.

II

"HOW TO DRAW," AND OTHER SUNDRY MATTERS

It is not bright colors but good drawing that makes figures beautiful. —TITIAN

To know how to draw is not to draw well. —GAUGUIN

L'exactitude n'est pas la vérité. —MATISSE

At last I do not know how to draw any more. —TOULOUSE-LAUTREC

"Van Gogh," said a popular and financially successful portrait painter recently, "was a serious but clumsy artist; why, he didn't know how to draw!" This is a surprisingly tenacious notion; one even hears it said of Picasso. The fact is that both men knew very well how to draw (see Plates 1 and 2): Van Gogh had an astonishing command of his medium, and Picasso is one of the most felicitous draftsmen of the entire Western tradition.

In explaining excellence in art, the criterion of "good drawing" has been appealed to for centuries by layman and patron and critic alike—and by none more vehemently than the artist himself. Michelangelo felt that Titian could color but not draw, and Ingres felt very much the same about Delacroix. (Both Michelangelo and Ingres were wrong.) In our day, painters (many of whom work in an "abstract" medium) grow very excited about the proper teaching of drawing, but I have found it

Collection, Museum of Modern Art, New York. Abby Aldrich Rockefeller Bequest

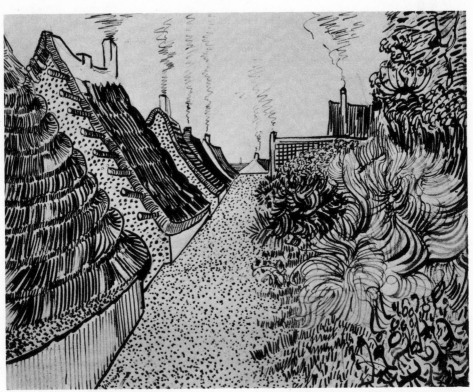

PLATE 1: Vincent van Gogh, *Streets in Saintes-Maries*, 1888. Reed pen and ink, 9⅝″ x 12½″

PLATE 2: Pablo Picasso, *Four Ballet Dancers*, 1925. Pen and ink, 13⅞″ x 10″

Collection, Museum of Modern Art, New York. Gift of Abby Aldrich Rockefeller

difficult, even by cross-examination, to find out exactly what most of them mean.

One could start with the premise that in an important sense drawing is the origin of all the visual arts. The architect does not build; he conceives. And his conceptions are rendered in drawings. It was *plans* (not houses) by the young Frank Lloyd Wright that excited and influenced the abstract painting of Piet Mondrian. Similarly in sculpture, drawing is almost always used at some point in order to establish scale, contour and position, as well as the relationship of front to side and front to back. The graphic arts (woodcut, engraving, etching, etc.) have developed as extensions of drawing. And while painting may or may not proceed directly from drawing, there is hardly a known instance of a painter who did not make drawings and consider them an important way of developing his ideas.

So considered, drawing becomes an initial way of art-thinking, setting forth the identity and form of a building, engraving, fresco, carving, or for that matter, of a musical composition. And even *outside* art—in mathematics, engineering, warfare or statecraft—drawing is a primary way of thinking. (We speak of "drawing" plans for an attack, "drafting" a constitution or an economic project.) In art this conceptual function of drawing is sometimes underrated. The final painting or sculpture will impress by size, body, color, material or placement; but it is often in the drawing that the artist's thinking is most clearly and unequivocably presented. Painters will allow that in painting they can sometimes get away with effects they could not in drawing; drawing thus serves as a check as well as a plan. It is not at all inconceivable that in our age of more specialized artistic functions there will be a resurgence of drawing as a finished art form, a form which states the final thought without compromise or seduction and so imposes itself despite an unimposing size or medium.

But what does it mean to argue that Van Gogh can or cannot "draw"?

Theoretical or dictionary meanings aside, the concept of drawing has a very real meaning in art, perhaps all the more because artists hesitate to define it. Degas once said, "Draw lines, young man, and still more lines, both from life and from memory."

A modern drawing well illustrating the use of lines from life and memory is Paul Klee's *Limits of Understanding* (Plate 3). The effect is comparable to a musical counterpoint in which a simplicity of means (here, sharp lines and soft mists) produces a surprising complexity of combinations and suggestions. The drawing would have to be called abstract; yet it carries connotations of experiences meaningful enough to modern man.

In the lower center of the drawing are two cone-shaped images which seem to suggest light converging and diverging through a prism or plane; the two cones terminate in something resembling human eyes, although one "eye" looks like a concentric diagram with geometric significance, and the other, like part of a continuum of light, perhaps the lens of a flashlight. The rays or lines then continue as in elements of an electric filament. Underneath are two incisive, sweeping arcs which might suggest calipers—or astral paths.

Working in and around these features are networks of lines—now open, now more nearly closed; now cutting through each other, now overlapping; now making static patterns, now traveling away. Toward the bottom of the drawing these lines tend to converge in shapes which provide stability, as of cornerstones, including one pyramidal complex, which though highly stable in itself, is then transformed into lines of direction.

As these networks of lines move higher they come together in climbing, sometimes rooflike forms, and finally in what appears to be a series of ladders, or a fire escape, or part of an aerial contraption suspended from a great balloon. But the balloon might also be a sun or moon (both dark and light at once), or again a great eye without a cornea; the

PLATE 4: Edgar Degas, Dancers, circa 1899. Pastel, 37¼″ x 31¾″

PLATE 3: Paul Klee, *Limits of Understanding*, 1927. Drawing

missing cornea, however, is supplied in the eyelike form with which our voyage began.

This large circular body is denser, and thus heavier, than anything below. At the same time it seems suspended in infinite space, separated from the forms below by a misty cloud. But since it is of the same substance as the upper form, the cloud in turn acts as a medium between that and the others. In the misty area, enclosed within a sharp and regular line, the effect is of confinement; in the other it is mysterious, unconfined and thus undefined.

The mist emerges again in the lower right corner; this not only carries a unifying pattern across the picture, but picks up a specific echo in the pattern of lines adjacent to it, lines which crosshatch to make shaded tones. So throughout the drawing there is a play of open and closed shapes, of the defined and undefined, of lines felt as boundaries or directions, of tones versus marks. Sometimes the lines work singly, sometimes in pairs; when in pairs, they may run parallel or converge; when grouped, they may compose solid forms or flicker in delicate iridescence.

In addition to a variety of uses as an element of form, the line also ranges in its suggestion of cognitive experiences, from the optical to the electronic to the cosmological, and again in its connotation of human faculties, from visual and manual operations through vast possibilities of the eye and mind to new possibilities of synthesizing or reconstructing phenomena, and to a final aspiration which soars above the very "limits of understanding."

When a person tries to draw something—an object, a face, a figure—he usually seeks to establish its contours, its physical existence—hence, its identity. He may then say, Behold, I have drawn a horse! He has rendered a semblance of something out of nature upon a piece of paper. A laudable ambition; indeed, something of a miracle.

But if a man draws a horse, is it a horse he is making, or a drawing? Degas (Plate 4) said, "They call me a painter of dancers; they don't realize that for me the dancer has been a pretext for painting pretty materials and delineating movement." Here we take a step closer to learning what drawing is about. Degas is not drawing the dancer. She already exists; how could he make her more real on paper than she is in life? But he is stimulated by her, as he is by the "pretty materials," which also, however, he could not make more real than in life.

It is Degas' last dictum which gives the most helpful clue. He explains that he seeks to delineate movement. How simple this sounds, to "delineate movement"! Yet it is a contradiction in terms. To delineate is to draw, which in turn is to make marks, which when made, simply sit upon the page. They cannot move. Still, when looking at the drawing, one *feels* movement. Through some process, as mysterious as anything else in art, static forms have given birth to movement and the painting is somehow *alive*.

This process is not tied to the representation of objects. While the Degas drawing represents dancers, the Jackson Pollock, which depicts pure rhythm, creates its own dance.

Placing several drawings together—the Degas, the Van Gogh, the Picasso, the Gorky (Plate 5) and the Pollock (Plate 6)—it is easy to see that a line is not simply a line; it is always becoming something else: the lines in the Degas become shadings, tones and patches; in the Van Gogh they become dashes, dots and hatchings; the Picasso lines make rhythmic contours; in the Gorky, they make shapes, tones and touches; and in the Pollock: a meandering substance that widens and thickens, narrows and almost disappears. If line can mean so many things, then what, in this more technical sense, does drawing boil down to?

The most elementary act of the draftsman, I should propose, is to

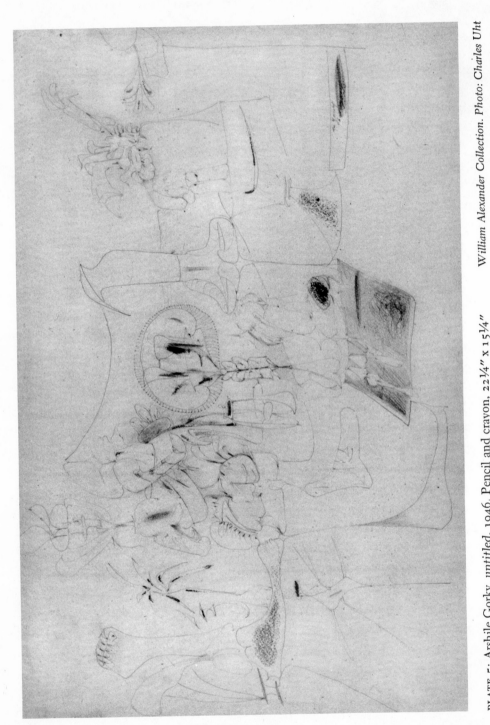

PLATE 5: Arshile Gorky, untitled, 1946. Pencil and crayon, 22¼″ x 15¼″   *William Alexander Collection. Photo: Charles Uht*

make a mark. Line itself may be thought of as a series of marks or as one mark continued and developed. Ultimately it is the mark that distinguishes painting from drawing, no idle distinction. Painting is involved in surfaces, in over-all effects. Drawing makes marks, and it is this marking which unites the abstract aspects (lines, rhythms, accents) with the thematic aspects (the idea, the way of thinking). To mark the paper is to mark down one's thoughts.

In a painting the artist may show his hand through the character of his color or shapes, his brushwork or handling of paint. In a drawing the artist shows his hand in the character of the marking. And so the mark has a calligraphic significance: it is like a signature.

Drawing has a further significance, which is involved in the art of composition. An older meaning of drawing was based on the Italian term *disegno*, which incorporated the concepts of designing and composing. Thus, in Renaissance art, drawing was directed first to the design of figure or object, then to the composing of the entire picture. Drawing was in charge of working out the functions of the different parts and ultimately the over-all scheme.

This function is very important to remember today, when "good drawing" is so frequently invoked to mean *depicting*. "Learn to draw!" say advertisements of the commercial schools. What does this mean? Almost always: learn how to draw a cow or a tree or the nude figure or a chair or a city street or a face. A popular book on learning to draw presents as its chapter headings: "Perspective," "Composition," "Heads and Portraits," "Anatomy and Action," "Figure Drawing," "How to Draw Animals," "How to Sketch Children," "Trees and Landscapes."

Only the chapter entitled "Composition" refers to anything that is not simply rendering, but this chapter is disqualified also because its subtitle, "How to arrange your subjects for an interesting effect," suggests what is done with flowers or furniture. "Arranging" would involve the manipulation of things that are already complete in themselves. As opposed to composition, this is an exceedingly limited concept of drawing.

I have not cited these chapter headings in order to disparage a highly skilled and knowledgeable profession, but rather to suggest that these ideas about drawing (and thus in many ways about art itself) are widely held by the layman. While arrangement may have an important place in the art of drawing, it by no means tells what drawing is about. And as for depiction, indeed it was a commercial artist, the poster designer Maurice Logan, who warned that "in commercial art, anatomical perfection is not the important thing; it is the rhythm of the finished production that counts."

How often is the layman disturbed by what he feels to be "distortions" in modern art—or, to be more specific, in modern idioms of drawing? But *all* art is distortion. Michelangelo and Raphael always distorted, and merely in a different way and to a different purpose than Van Gogh or Picasso. Even literature, the art most directly involved with life, distorts by its very nature, which is to fictionalize. Does a good book transcribe what people say in the actual words that people speak? To do so would be quite unconvincing. When people talk they use pauses, intonations, volumes, pitches, resonances, accentuations and so on, not to mention gestures, all of which have to be interpreted, evaluated and put into an entirely new form in the written word. Herein lies the art, or at least a part of it. To be sure, it is necessary to have a good ear in order to write people's speech. Similarly, it is necessary to have a good eye in order to draw people's actions. But these are only means, and more than that, only means toward certain kinds of art. To the commercial writer or painter, skill in both observation and in rendering are crucial because either one is primarily telling a story.

In art and literature the story is incidental—only an incident, just as is the story in a parable. The truths of art and philosophy may deal to a greater or to a lesser extent with specific life situations, but they never end there. Where these truths do end is by no means the same, of course, in modern art as in older art, and for this reason it is important, in coming to grips with modern art, to see what it does *not* seek to do.

One thing modern art refuses to do is to draw a thing literally, the way it appears. I say "literally" because there is no definitive way in which to draw an object. All representational drawing proceeds according to certain conventions, which are in themselves oversimplifications of the impossibly complex and changing ways in which one actually sees. These conventions are quite arbitrary and depend in large part on cultural values.

Compare, for example, the rendering of the human figure by Classical Greek artists and by Western artists of the Renaissance, both of whom were interested in the nude figure objectively and as an ideal. The Classical artist gave the figure a predominance of long muscles; the Western artist tended to render them much shorter. Presumably there was no significant difference in body type between the ancient Greek and Renaissance Italian; and in any case, anatomically speaking, the length of a muscle never varies much.

Since these art forms worked close to the model, what caused these impressive differences in formal emphasis? Largely cultural values. The Classical civilization was based upon leisure, ease, grace, harmony and repose; Western civilization, to which the Renaissance belongs, prefers a system of dynamics—energy, movement, thrust. The instinctive choice of the artists unconsciously expresses these preferences.

The modern artist refuses to depict an object according to any given convention precisely because he feels that the convention appeals to a kind of previous knowledge, and not to a true experiencing of the thing. Thus, it is toward an ever more direct, more immediate or more "existential" experiencing of life that modern art has pointed.

When the Impressionists (Color Plate 1) refused to draw according to natural proportion and perspective (or at least according to previous conventions), they were not refusing to paint things as they are. They were insisting that what a person sees is not necessarily what he expected to see—things need not look as they have always been "pictured." By refusing to accept proportion and foreshortening and perspective as such, the Impressionists were able to see a whole new world of light, color and tone. Of these they made both a great art and a new mode of vision, from which in turn their followers made a convention. When operating in a convention, one is largely prevented from making a new discovery. This is why Impressionism had to come and why it had to go.

With this feeling about convention, modern art entered a series of stages which follow logically one from the other. The attitudes, values and decisions of contemporary artists have a background of five or six or seven generations. Artists from Goya to the present have been more interested in how man sees things and what he feels about them than in the way things literally look—in their substance, measurement and proportion—which was of prime interest to earlier artists.

When Albrecht Dürer or Leonardo da Vinci thought about how to draw, they thought about depicting people and objects and establishing spatial interrelationships, which often involved them in scientific investigations. Such objective analysis does not account for the art in their work, but it does account for much of the motivation. One of the ends of art is revelation, and this may take the form of scientific discovery quite as well as inner vision.

An artist may profit from trying to make a very close copy of an old-master drawing—say a Leonardo or a Dürer—because of the eloquence of the *ideas*, involving representation, structure, form, composition. But when he tries to copy an Ingres or a Van Gogh or a Seurat or a Matisse drawing, he is up against a near impossibility. The aesthetic ideas involved in modern drawing have become so personal as to be almost

PLATE 6: Jackson Pollock, *untitled*, 1951. Ink on paper, 18″ x 24″

inimitable; modern man has a predilection for unique experience. However, the generality or the uniqueness of an artistic experience does not
necessarily have anything to do with its communicability.

When the modern artist thinks about how to draw, he is less likely to
think of meticulous rendering than of a knowledge and command of his
medium sufficient to facilitate whatever expression he is moved toward.
And here lies another widespread misconception about modern art.

In saying that an artist "really can draw" (or paint or write), one may
be referring entirely to his technical facility. Technique in itself can be
exciting, and therefore it can be an important element in art. But the
skill of the juggler to entertain should not be confused with the power of
the creative artist to move. And technical skill in itself does not necessarily identify the artist. Picasso is more skilled at drawing—in the sense of
dexterity, facility, manual articulation—than either Raphael or
Cézanne, but he is not a greater maker of drawings. Swinburne was more
felicitous with words than many a greater writer. But as Hemingway
observed, "Few great authors have a brilliant command of language."

So while the felicity of technical skill has a distinct value, it must be
kept in its place. In the Renaissance, sheer artistry was considered a
delightful embellishment, a commendable eloquence further refining
the theatrical presentation. In modern abstract art, where the exploitation of the more purely aesthetic factors in drawing or painting (that is,
line, shape, color, paint manipulation and so on) becomes part of the
subject matter, skill *as such* has rightly become suspect. Since it is
essential to give a context to these aesthetic components, the modern
artist rejects artistry when it is used for its own sake.

One cannot begin to appreciate the painting of Vincent van Gogh or
Henri Matisse or Jackson Pollock without first appreciating that despite
widespread notions to the contrary, these modern artists did indeed

know how to draw, and to reapply the words of W.S. Gilbert, "They did it very well."

If painting cannot be understood apart from drawing, what exactly is the function of drawing in relation to painting? In the Renaissance, drawing was preliminary to painting. The sketch, the study, the plan and the cartoon (a full-scale working drawing for a large painting) all proceeded in a series of steps toward the final realization of the painting, whether frescoed wall or complex composition in oil. The drawing belonged to the workshop of the artist and was not meant for public view.

Rembrandt, working in the later Renaissance, was probably the first major artist to offer his drawings for sale as independent works of art. Still, no one considered them final statements in the sense that his more studied etchings or oil paintings were final. On through the eighteenth century, drawing remained primarily a background for painting. Only in the modern age—with the wash and charcoal drawings of Goya, the line and tone drawings of Ingres, the wash drawings of Constable or the water colors of Turner—did the art of drawing take on a new function. (As a result, the drawings of old masters, such as Rembrandt, are now looked upon as an independent genre, with their own authority.)

This is not to say that drawing is *as* important as painting, though it has probably become equal to graphics (printmaking), which was not true in the Renaissance. More significant than the varying importance of drawing in modern art is its independence. In the Renaissance a work of art was essentially a visual idea. It might be expressed in any medium—drawing, printmaking, painting or even sculpture. The medium was just that—a context. In modern art the medium has a larger role, according to which its own qualities become part of the subject. The medium has thus become a controlling factor. Painters still make drawings both as studies for and studies after their own paintings, just as they always have. But the art of drawing, during the past two centuries, has developed its

Sidney Janis Gallery, New York. Photo: Eric Pollitzer

own autonomy, its own reason for being. Drawing has become not only a way of thinking, but a way of expressing—and one distinct from painting.

Consider a black and white painting by Franz Kline (Plate 7). The work is composed, to a great degree, of strokes "drawn" on the canvas. It has no color, an element ordinarily associated with painting. It makes extensive use of marks, edges, shapes, accentuations—all of which are associated with drawing.

Should this painting therefore be called a drawing? Certainly not. Though also a wonderful maker of drawings, Kline was very much a painter, and this is a work that could not have been executed, or even conceived, except as a painting.

Is this because of its size? Not directly, for some paintings can be very small, and some drawings rather large. You can draw with a brush or paint with a stick. And drawings, like this painting, can be executed on canvas (and paintings on paper).

Is it possible to argue that this painting is a painting because its blacks and whites actually function as colors? Many painters would think so. One can argue that with painters such as Giorgione, Zurbarán or the contemporary Giorgio Cavallon (Color Plate 6), white attains a color function; or that with painters such as Velasquez, Manet or Kline, the same is true of black. Such an argument has some merit, for it emphasizes the extraordinary *sense* of substance, tangibility and range of value (lightness and darkness) in these blacks and whites.

Further, this interpretation agrees with the idea that a painting must have color. Accordingly, even Kasimir Malevich's *White on White* (Plate 8) is a color painting, even a treatise on color. Technically, however, black and white (and all the intermediary shades of gray) are *values*, and color is present only when there is *hue* (red, yellow and blue, and the various mixtures that can be produced from these primary colors).

Having weighed these considerations, it is now possible to make a

PLATE 7: Franz Kline, *Slate Cross*, 1961. Oil on canvas, 9′3″ x 79″

serviceable distinction between the art of painting and of drawing. A painting may be executed with any instruments and may be with or without color in the sense of hue. It may be on paper, wood, canvas, glass, even stone or metal, and it may employ almost any material (tempera, oil, plaster, wax or water), but *this material must be used so that its substance and surface (in relation to the canvas, or other ground) are major aesthetic factors.* Thus, a tiny Sienese panel, a huge Florentine fresco, a Byzantine mosaic of glass or a Roman mosaic of stone, a cardboard sketch by Toulouse-Lautrec or a vast compilation of oil, duco, sand and glass by Jackson Pollock all belong to the art of painting.

A drawing follows this definition up to a certain point. But unlike a painting, a drawing may not use its material to produce the effect of substance—though its quality will often play a role.

The most typical kind of modern painting—the Cézanne, the Matisse, the De Kooning or Kline—paints itself. By this I mean that though the artist may have some very specific ideas as to the kind of picture he intends to make, the painting he eventually creates is the product of a complex process of working with and *in* the painting, reworking it; adjusting it within itself, sometimes actually repainting the entire surface a number of times.

This is an entirely different process from the typical procedure in the Renaissance, where a picture was already final in the artist's mind before he began to paint, and the process of development had already taken place in a series of preliminary sketches and studies. Thus, the development in an older painting is embodied in a number of separate works. The modern painting embodies its own development.

It might be tempting to use the word "picture" for the Renaissance work, and "painting" for the modern. The distinction is, I think, a good one. A Renaissance picture actually depicts a scene, one that can be read as a story or visualized as a theatrical set. It denotes an object world. Whether its cast of characters is people, trees or wine jugs, these are treated as definable objects. But the whole tendency of modern painting has been toward seeing an object less and less in terms of the absolute fact of its existence, more and more in terms of its interaction with its environment. In the nineteenth century this environment took the form of external nature, but in the twentieth century the environment is what goes on within the painting itself. At the same time the depicted object has been relinquished; the painting itself has become the object.

It is the painting then as an act—or as a complex of actions and decisions—presented in the painter's private language, which distinguishes the contemporary work. This aspect did, of course, exist in the Renaissance—especially in the later and bolder works of Titian and Tintoretto, El Greco and Rembrandt—but it was subordinate to the main goal, the development of the painting *as a picture*. It does not make much sense to refer to a modern painting, at least to any really important work since Cézanne, as a picture; on the other hand, to insist upon calling a contemporary painting a *painting* emphasizes one of its essential characteristics, and goes in fact to the heart of its being.

Increasingly that "being" is a matter of becoming. "The significance of a work of art is determined . . . by the quality of its growth," Hans Hofmann has said, and quite clearly he had modern painting in mind. The world not as established or finite fact, but as *process*—this is the outlook which separates the modern artist and scientist alike from the Renaissance artist and philosopher. For while the Renaissance knew the world as static and determinable, the modern age finds reality in constant flux, in the indeterminable.

Since art is at once a source and product of its age, modern art could no more share the values of Renaissance art than modern science could be Newtonian, or modern statecraft dynastic. It is still sometimes argued that Picasso would paint like Raphael if he could. The fact is that

Picasso in a technical sense could, and in a cultural sense could not, paint like Raphael. And the corollary is that were Raphael at work today, he would be a very different painter from what he was in the sixteenth century. This is also apparent if applied to John Milton or Abraham Lincoln, to Karl Marx or Henry James.

A world of visualized objects located in a measurable space was strictly a Renaissance creation. Why does anyone assume that this is the only proper subject matter of art? The wonderful painting styles of the Middle Ages cared little for visualized objects and nothing for measurable space; the general tendency of art since the end of the eighteenth century has been to reject such a world as inappropriate. For the modern age, which has increasingly come to recognize its own values and is perhaps only now really grasping the problems of its own exclusive identity, the old approach may have interest, but little meaning.

The belief that "what we touch is more real than what we see" (which one distinguished critic cited as the essence of drawing) helps chiefly when explaining Renaissance art, which above all sought the tangible. Its vast and continuous studies of perspective and foreshortening, its anatomical or botanical inquiries, are all attempts to translate into visual terms what we know by actual touch of the sensory world. Renaissance painting and sculpture sought to create a substitute image of a real, tangible, knowable object. Thus, one contemplates the Mona Lisa as an actual woman. But when Matisse was told that the woman in one of his paintings did not look like a woman, he replied, "That is not a woman, it's a painting."

Contrast this with the Renaissance painter-historian Vasari's tale of Giotto and the fly. Giotto, "when he was still a boy, and studying with Cimabue, once painted a fly on the nose of a figure on which Cimabue himself was working, and this so naturally that when the master returned to continue his work, he believed it to be real and lifted his hand more than once to drive it away before he would go on with the

PLATE 8: Kasimir Malevich, *Suprematist* Composition: White on White, 1918?
Oil on canvas, 31¼″ x 31¼″

painting." Or lest this be considered an incidental love of trickery, consider Donatello's attitude toward his Zuccone (an intensively lifelike statue), of which it was said that while he was working on it he would exclaim, "Speak then! why wilt thou not speak?"

This Pygmalion motive in art is essentially Classical or Renaissance, just as the idea of a holy spirit incarnate in an image can be found in many times and places—in Egyptian portraiture, for example, or many kinds of primitive statuary, or Russian icons. Matisse's attitude is specifically modern.

When Raphael wanted to paint a beautiful woman, he would, as he said, combine the perfect nose of one woman, the perfect brow of another, the neck of a third and the eyes or limbs of still another. Thinking of woman as woman in this way might be called thinking *in things*. Georges Braque, one of the most classically minded artists of our century, has said, "I do not believe in things: I believe only in their relationships, in their circumstances." Here lies the vital difference. Raphael believed in the concrete present existence of things, and he expressed this belief in all his art. Braque, like a modern scientist or behaviorist, cannot separate a thing from its relationships, its circumstances, its environment.

Since it is this *field of experience* that is vitally meaningful to man, the separable object is not merely inexpressive, it is a positive hindrance to expression. For this reason, and not out of mere caprice, the relentless succession of painters from Goya to Jackson Pollock have increasingly rejected the figure or object as such. A critic, Pierre Schneider, has rightly said that "it is the figurative image that roots and immobilizes a painting." To be "immobile" is fatal to any work of art, since one criterion is that it be alive.

But what is wrong with being "rooted"? Some styles, such as most Greek or Egyptian art, depend very much on this sensation. However, the sense of the modern lies in dynamics. A static art form is outside our context, and even with an artist such as Mondrian (Plate 18), despite superficial appearances, there is much that is not static. While the basic elements appear immobile and defined in themselves (vertical and horizontal lines making squares and rectangles which enclose primary colors and black and white), the way in which they interact is vibrant and full of contrasts. By opening out toward almost all its edges, the painting expands. The colors are kept in place, in balance with one another and the force of the patterns, by dynamic tensions of this spatial push and pull. Indeed, it is these very qualities—dynamics, cohesiveness and intensity—which distinguish a Mondrian from an imitation.

The layman is apt to say, "What I want in a painting is something I can recognize." The modern artist has not, I think, rejected the "recognition" nearly so much as the "something." All art has to do with recognizing; that is, all visual art. But whether what one recognizes is an external object or an internal vision—here lies a drastic difference.

The modern artist may reject the object for several reasons: first, the basic shift from the static, tangible world of the Renaissance to the dynamic, relativist world of the twentieth century; second, the persistent tendency of modern art to be more purely and professionally art—to repudiate, for example, any connection with other disciplines. Today art deals in emotion perhaps more than in any other element in human experience. One is "moved" by a book, a play, a symphony—or he is not. Similarly, he is moved by a painting, and the quality of this emotion may or may not depend upon "'something" he "recognized" in the picture. Professor John Fairbank has warned that the "Chinese [artist] does not deal with a material, mechanical world . . . He depicts not what he sees but what he feels." And this applies no less to modern art.

In certain important respects, modern art (meaning art since Goya) is closer to the styles of the Middle Ages than to those of the intervening Renaissance and Baroque—a rapport that has been noted by historians as well as felt by artists, who have long shown a tendency to tack photographs of Romanesque sculpture or Gothic glass in their studios. Behind this interest lies a mutual rejection of proportion and perspective and the static, earth-bound classical form. Both medieval and modern art repudiate any real kinship with scientific theory or procedure.

In particular, one may observe such a rapport in the echoes of old art forms—of illuminated (illustrated) manuscripts in the works of Paul Klee, of the late medieval woodcut in modern Expressionism, or in the revival of the triptych (the three-part Gothic altarpiece) in the work of Max Beckmann (Plate 27) and others.

The rejections mentioned above have a positive purpose, shared by both the medieval and the modern age: an emphasis on the *surface* of the painting as an arena in which passages develop, and also as a surface in itself wherein qualities of the paint as tone and as substance are worked out. Naturally there are elements of all these qualities in Renaissance painting—indeed, in any painting, as distinguished from drawing. But in Renaissance painting, such elements are subordinated to the representation of form and the illusion of space.

Both medieval and modern art reject the depiction of proportioned figures and measured objects in a preconceived space. Simultaneously both tend to develop, in greater or less degree, an *abstraction of form in order to express emotive content*, which was seldom permitted in the Renaissance world. It would not be far-fetched to say that the major trend in the art of the past quarter century, Abstract Expressionism, clearly recalls the abstraction and expressionism which distinguished later medieval art, and that it thereby reunites two of the most fundamental aesthetic experiences of the West.

This is not to suggest that modern art is a reversion to the art of the Middle Ages. For in many other respects they are profoundly different. Modern Art is the most art-conscious style in the history of the West, while Romanesque and Gothic art were the least so. Modern art is the most personal and the least systematically symbolic (i.e., no formal set of symbols). It is the freest from prescribed authority, the most experimental, the most solipsistic, the most problematical. Modern art belongs to the studio and the museum; medieval art belonged to cathedral and castle. Modern art is above all the concern of the individual artist and collector; medieval art was primarily the concern of church and society. Modern art deals in states of mind and spirit; medieval art dealt in saints and devils.

"An artist paints so that he will have something to look at," said the contemporary painter Barnett Newman. This statement is more poignant than it may at first look. It suggests that the modern artist creates his own visual environment, which was not at all the case with either the Renaissance or the Gothic artist. The Gothic artist painted so that God might see his testimonial and devotion; the Renaissance artist, so that men might see their world. The modern artist paints in order to see himself.

In this connection it is helpful to consider again the idea of the modern painting as a process. This idea reveals something about the nature of the painting and its intrinsic values, but it also says something about the modern artist. While he is painting, the modern artist is totally involved in the work. Both the medieval and the Renaissance artist proceeded according to certain formulas, which, when worked out in relation to the particular painting, permitted the artist to execute his work with a certain ease and without the need to make an issue of every passage, much less every stroke. In contrast, "every stroke an issue" might be one way of defining the essence of the best modern painting.

One could easily imagine the Renaissance painter thinking of all sorts of other matters while he was actually painting; that is, he could lead a life outside his art. The modern artist does so at his peril. The genuine modern artist (as distinguished from the imitator, the man with a trick to catch the public eye or the mere manufacturer of paintings) will spend enormous and often agonizing periods of studio time in pure "gestation." In this aspect of his life he may (or may not) be very much involved in politics, literature, sports, philosophy—conceivably even in art criticism. But when he is in a painting, and the phrase is used advisedly, he is more involved—in body and mind, emotion and spirit—than the earlier type of artist. I say "type" because one may well think of the later works of Michelangelo or Rembrandt as proceeding in this personally involved manner, and among all older art it is just such works which for us today seem the most "modern."

Since the contemporary painter does not follow a preconceived plan, he is faced with a problem which did not ordinarily beset the earlier artists: he has to decide when he is finished. Picasso has remarked that to know when to stop is the whole secret of painting. But how does the artist know when this point is reached. Borrowing from artists' language, one would answer that when a painting really "works," when it works the way he wants it to, this is the time to stop.

In any case, the problem is never-ending, a truly aesthetic problem of as serious an order as the relation between perspective and formal composition was for the Renaissance. Jackson Pollock spoke what is perhaps the final word on the subject. When a sympathetic visitor asked, "But Mr. Pollock, how do you know when you've finished?" the artist replied, "Madam, how do you know when you've finished making love?"

III

SOME MISCONCEPTIONS
AND HOW TO DEAL WITH THEM

A genius can soar to dizzying heights and delve to depths inaccessible to his contemporaries. But he cannot step out of the time into which he is born. —CURT SACHS

We have to comprehend the artist's own values, and only then are fit to pronounce any judgment. —HAVELOCK ELLIS

I do not read English, an English book is a blank book to me. This does not mean that the English language does not exist, and why should I blame anybody but myself if I cannot understand what I know nothing about? —PABLO PICASSO

"The representata of art [that is, the objects represented] do service as the words of language. The formal arrangement is the grammar and syntax. The aesthetic emotion is the meaning," says the distinguished art historian Rhys Carpenter. This sounds reasonable, and indeed, can be of some help in the appreciation of Classical Greek sculpture, for example, or certain kinds of Renaissance painting. But what good is it applied to a Byzantine icon, where the representation of the Virgin is inseparable from the emotion and the "meaning"? Is the statement true of a Persian rug, a Celtic manuscript with little or no "representata," or a painting by Jean Dubuffet, not to mention Mark Rothko?

I do not wish to debate with Professor Carpenter, but to suggest that no description of the aesthetics of painting has yet been made which has more than a rather limited application. This is not to say that one shouldn't seek descriptions, even definitions, or perhaps above all, vital parallels between one kind of experience and another. "We find it hard to believe what lies beyond our understanding," La Rochefoucauld said, and one of the commonest ways of broadening understanding is by the use of analogy.

Granting that there may be an advantage in comparing the art of painting to arts with which the reader happens to be more familiar, what analogies are the most useful? The answer cannot be clear-cut, because the analogy changes; different analogies are significant at different times. This is a fact which art critics and historians might ponder and investigate more often.

For example, the frescoes and vase paintings of the ancient Greeks are probably best illuminated by an analogy with the art of carved sculpture. In approaching most Gothic painting, however, the best analogy is with architecture. Architecture in turn is no help in illuminating the character of most Renaissance painting. In the fifteenth century an analogy with sculpture (stone in Italy, wood in the North) is again very helpful, but in the sixteenth, seventeenth and eighteenth centuries it is probably literature that gives the best introduction to painting.

By the nineteenth century the attempt to tell a story in paint was usually disastrous. Goya still, and even Delacroix, could pull it off, but the Pre-Raphaelite Brotherhood was doomed in its attempts to reintroduce a perennial English taste for literature into painting. At the same time, a large proportion of academic painting succumbed to the enticements of storytelling.

A special kind of storytelling is found in the portrait; it tells the story of a personality, and, in the greatest portraits, of a soul. From the early Renaissance through the eighteenth century, portraiture was as important as any other subject in painting. For the next hundred years the portrait still held its head up, but during the course of the nineteenth century it steadily declined both in frequency of appearance and in importance assigned to it by the major artists. That this was not primarily due to the invention of photography is pretty clear from the fact that landscape subjects (equally accessible to the camera) remained at least as numerous even as the portrait declined.

One still hears that photography has radically affected the history of painting. It is sometimes presumed, for example, that the fact that more interesting portraiture has been done by photographers than by painters in this century is due merely to the availability and speed of the camera. And further, that had photography been available during the Renaissance, it would have replaced painting and sculpture as the medium for making portraits.

I say "making" portraits rather than "rendering" because any significant portrait is a created image, not just a simulation. In the great age of European portraiture—from Van Eyck to Van Gogh—is it conceivable that any major painter or sculptor would have been satisfied with the flatness, the accidentalness, the superficiality—indeed, the "objectivity" —of the photograph? The true portrait has a metaphysical value; one of its prime functions is, as Renaissance man proclaimed, no less than to conquer death. To accomplish this, an image must be created, and the making of an image requires the combined and inspired operation of the hand and mind, the will and understanding, the vision and grasp of the creative artist.

Is it not curious that while photography was available for more than half of the nineteenth century, it rarely supplanted painting in serious portraiture? And in landscape, the nineteenth century, one of the greatest of all ages of outdoor studies, took almost no notice of the photograph. Styles in photography have tended to follow—at a distance of something like half a generation—the major styles in painting.

The camera can record, and its operator can select, but in the end the photographer is limited to manipulation. For this reason, photography has never been significant in the history of works of the imagination, works that create images and have worlds of their own. On the other hand, a wide variety of photographic effects have been useful and stimulating as *ingredients* in various forms of modern art, especially Dada, Surrealism and contemporary Pop and Op—styles that are themselves more involved in manipulative effects than in images produced by the creative imagination.

If literature (in the sense of storytelling) no longer serves as a useful analogy toward the understanding of modern painting, is there an art that does?

Mondrian thought that his art (which is among the most significant forms of our century) was moving toward the condition of architecture. It is hard to see this. Art and architecture have been largely independent of each other since the late eighteenth century. During the Renaissance both painting and architecture were chiefly involved in the creation of images. In the modern age, however, architecture has become an engineering art, though often imposing and at times a true aesthetic activity, as in Frank Lloyd Wright's creations of spatial experiences. But it is painting, and to a lesser degree sculpture, that have continued the role of imagery-making.

Wright's influence on Mondrian was not in his buildings, but in his drawn plans. And Mondrian's own influence on architecture was much less than his influence on design and commercial art. It seems to me a sheer misconception—held by Mondrian, by many critics and by some architects and architectural historians—that Mondrian's painting and modern painting in general are analogous to architecture.

What art, then, does modern painting most nearly resemble? The answer has to be music: instrumental music, especially as that art form has emerged in the West from the sixteenth to the twentieth century. The apprehension that painting was approaching the condition of music was testified to by some painters and writers as early as the eighteenth century. It is time for art criticism to face and exploit the immense possibilities of this analogy. Incidentally, the analogy can work both ways: K.P.E. Bach once called his fellow composer, Georg Telemann, "a great painter."

The similarity between modern painting and instrumental music is evidenced first in the fact that both tend to be abstract rather than literary or programmatic; that is, they reach their final statements of emotional truth, value and experience chiefly through the instruments of their own medium, and they do so directly, without trying to suggest specific or recognizable situations. The concert music of Arcangelo Corelli, Ludwig van Beethoven or Béla Bartók is thus, in painting terms, a kind of "abstract expressionism."

The fact that the literary mode is no longer pertinent to painting has been observed by many modern artists. More than a century ago Delacroix noted that he found in painting "a pleasure very different from the pleasure we find in a work of literature." Cézanne maintained that "the artist . . . must beware of the literary spirit which so often causes painting to deviate from its true path." And Matisse looked for a "living harmony of tones, a harmony not unlike that of a musical composition."

Since Renaissance painting was quite at home in telling a story, why shouldn't modern painting be? The only answer appears to be nothing less than a law of history: within the context of modern art, painting must logically evolve from a condition analogous to literature to a condition analogous to music. The increasing resemblance of painting to music was already clear to Edgar Allan Poe, as shown in his essay "The Poetic Principle," to Whistler in his essay "The Ten O'Clock Lecture," to Gauguin in a number of remarks. Writing in an early notebook, Joan Miró set the aim as *atenuyar la música*—to achieve music.

Modern painters frequently adopt musical terminology or practice, often in the very titles of their paintings. Whistler's *Nocturnes* and

Arrangements are examples, as is Abraham Walkowitz's *Color Symphony* (1916). Other contemporaries prefer numbering their pictures to naming them, another practice borrowed from music.

Kandinsky is not alone in having written of the "musical" aspects of color; he spoke of "the deep relations among the arts, and especially between music and painting." And it is not only color, but many facets, from drawing technique to total composition, in modern painting which can be described, characterized and evaluated through the terminology of music. One can make excellent use of such concepts as harmony, counterpoint, orchestration and even "composition"; such patterns as dissonance and discord, crescendo or diminuendo, sequence and progression; or such qualities as tone, pace, timbre, resonance or improvisation —all taken from music.

"Art is not imitation, but illusion," said Charles Reade. If it is possible to make a brief, sweeping statement about the art of painting, this one will serve. The idea that art is imitation is venerated among aestheticians. Left with them, it does relatively little harm, but among laymen it is probably the biggest single obstacle to the understanding of art.

To ask that a painting look like something is to ask that it should look like *something else*; that is, something other than a painting. I do not mean that a painting has artistic value only as the sum of its colors and forms—then it would be mere decoration. The decorative value may play a role in art (it is an important part of the aesthetic value of Veronese, Matisse and Jackson Pollock, among others), or it may have less importance, as in Dürer's engravings or most of the earlier Cubist paintings.

By the same token, the "representata"—the parts in a picture that look like something familiar—may or may not play an aesthetic role. In the painting of today there is a major cleavage between an art that wants to look very much like things in everyday life and an art that repudiates

PLATE 9: Willem de Kooning, *Woman*, 1950. Oil on canvas, 64″ x 46″

Weatherspoon Art Gallery Collection, University of North Carolina at Greensboro.
Lena Kernodle McDuffie Memorial Gift

both objects and imitations. Looking at the art of painting over the past thousand years, however, it is clear that while a style may or may not deal in imitations, it *always* deals in illusion. It is the indescribable illusion that transforms a good Impressionist painting (Color Plate 1) from an "imitation" of certain effects of sunlight into a creative vision —a work of art that summons up buried hopes and revives memories, that stirs both reminiscence and expectation, that presents a complete world which is richer, truer and more tender than we are ordinarily capable of finding for ourselves.

It is the unaccountable illusion that transforms the De Kooning (Plate 9) from a so-called woman who was originally a barfly into a prophetic and demonic force, an image apparently deep in the collective unconscious; and it also transforms the painting itself from agitations of pigment and color into a piling up of sunlit passages and stormy sweeps evocative of untamed snowy summits. The illusion which great art creates is somehow more real than real life. And this is why it is possible to say that art has life and a work of art has a capacity to "live."

Almost by definition, art gives us something new, something of greater value, something that we could *not* expect. It is therefore not so much mistaken as meaningless to say wistfully, "If only I could recognize something." There is a fine old song called "I like to recognize the tune." Why not? The tune was written to give pleasure in itself; whether it is played simply for its melody or to give the arranger or conductor an opportunity for improvisation is a matter of choice between performer and audience.

But when a painter chooses not to deal in recognizable objects, the spectator must take it or leave it. The painter is not working primarily to interest the spectator, but to satisfy himself. If he is a good painter and has satisfied himself, then the spectator owes it to *himself* not to seek in the work what he thought he wanted or expected. Art creates its own terms; there can be no compromises, no negotiations.

The layman has long sought to intrude his will into the creation of art. In the Renaissance it was the patron who interfered, but his effect has been somewhat overrated. Sometimes the lesser artists would follow instructions, but clearly Michelangelo paid no more attention to the Pope's ideas than it suited him to. In our own time the role of dictating style to the artist has fallen chiefly to some critics, some dealers and a few collectors. Again, only the lesser artists succumb to the blandishments of image or market.

This may sound as though the artist were saying, "The public be damned," but that isn't true at all. Unless he is a veritable misanthrope (which is less frequent in art than in some professions), the artist would desperately love to have people experience and understand his work. To paint purely to express oneself, purely for one's own satisfaction, is hardly meaningful except in a therapeutic sense. Art must have an individual meaning for the artist or it will have no motive, but it must also have a general, even a universal, meaning in terms of human experience: herein lies its eternal value.

So the artist wants his work to be known and experienced—but he prefers it to be approached in the right way. Picasso has warned that to take the picture from the easel can be the ruination of the painting, and Mark Rothko spoke for many an artist in saying, "It is a risky act to send a painting out into the world. How often it must be impaired by the eyes of the unfeeling and the cruelty of the impotent who would extend their affliction universally." The burden is on us to give the work its chance.

Is art a luxury? The answer is, of course: art is all sorts of things to all sorts of people. Still, it is a fact that in the Renaissance, art was widely held to be a basic to life, whereas in our own day it is more likely to be considered a luxury—by the public, that is, not by the serious artist. The Van Gogh or Jackson Pollock, for which a collector may have to put out a tenth of a million dollars in order to decorate his apartment, must seem to him a luxury, but to the artist this work is a necessity—to human life in general as well as his own.

Simply because modern art is sometimes considered a joke, it is important to remember that the best artists of our time think of their work as dealing in issues and values that border on the absolute and can be deadly serious. To be sure, a lot of jokes are perpetrated, both in good and bad faith. But the real problem is not the occasional joke—it's much more basic.

One basic misconception is to apply the producer-consumer relationship to art. One often hears the artist cast in the one role, the public in the other. But this applies to craft, not to art. It is precisely what distinguishes commercial art, no matter how effective, from "fine" art, however ineffective. Only in the most exceptional cases during the past century has a real artist worked on commission. If he even so much as has in mind a type of potential market, he is suspect with his fellows. The true artist produces for himself, not on demand.

Is a work of art consumed? It is not eaten up or worn out, and neither is it replaceable. If it is a significant work, its value increases rather than diminishes. Furthermore, the "consumer" cannot present his demands to the "producer"; he must take or leave what is offered. Clyfford Still is said to habitually select the one painting he decides he will show to a buyer (who must first secure an appointment); Vermeer operated in a similar manner in the seventeenth century. These are extremes, but revealing ones. In any case the modern artist almost always produces for himself; if someone wants to buy afterward, so much the better.

There is also a political misconception about modern art, which is usually expressed in talking of "conservative" and "radical" artists. What can this mean? In politics such labels can be useful because there is an established order and there are those who want to change it, sometimes radically. But in art there are only good and bad painters. If a man works in an outmoded style he will by definition do outmoded

PLATE 10: Pablo Picasso, *The Red Tablecloth*, 1924. Oil on canvas, 38¾" x 51⅜"

work; that is, it might be technically good, but it will have little meaning. Conversely, if a man carries experimentation in art beyond the point where he is dealing in vital issues, again his work will have little meaning. Art can have radical features or conservative values, but essentially it must, as Daumier said, be of its time. The concept of an "avant-garde" usually comes from the critic, as the idea of artistic "radicals" is supplied by the public.

The artist thinks of himself as following his own road, but only as he follows it does he discover where it leads. This is totally different from the political leader, whose function is to know precisely where he stands and what his stand implies. For the artist it is rather as Degas explained: "Only when he no longer knows what he is doing does the painter do good things."

Another problem involves a "social" misconception about modern art. According to this, we speak of the "success" and "failure" of a work, an artist or a style. Such terms work well enough when applied to a war, a baseball team, even to psychoanalytic treatment. But they have little application to art. Even if one could grant that there is such a thing as a perfect picture, as so great a critic as Lionello Venturi sometimes claimed, it is hard to demonstrate. And even if it could be demonstrated, one would have to admit that there are lesser, though perfect, works and greater imperfect ones.

More appropriate terms would be "effective" and "ineffective." If the painting works, if it is telling, if it has the power to affect life, then it has value: on the other hand, if it is brilliant, entertaining, skillful, surprising or charming, but in the end unconvincing, then it must be judged ineffective as art. Only in the sense that art succeeds in moving the viewer can it legitimately be associated with the idea of success, and even then it is usually difficult, sometimes impossible, to say *why* one is moved.

The "success" of a bridge is quite another matter. Even the success of a business or political career can often be pinpointed; we ask, What is the secret of So-and-so's success? But the secret of how Cézanne is able to move us so profoundly is the secret of art itself.

And another misconception: How often is it said that in a picture something has been "caught"? This picture need not be a portrait of a girl in the evanescence of youth, or a running horse, or a spectacular sunset; it might be a semiabstract depiction of a coastal storm or even an abstract Cubist painting in which it is claimed that a fourth dimension such as Time itself has been "caught." To capture even an essence of a moment or of a scene or of a human personality is surely valuable, but does it have anything to do with the function of art? When the artist has caught it, has he created a work of art or a memory stimulus?

The true function of art is not to catch something that already exists; it is to create something that never existed before. The cleverness of the hunter is not an important criterion; one should pay attention instead to true originality.

The next misconception may do more harm than is usually recognized. It seems clear that there are no absolute criteria by which one can tell whether a modern painting is good or bad, important or trivial. If there were, signs could be posted at the entrance to any gallery, and surely there would be no point in a book such as this. So one might conclude that the only useful test for an unfamiliar work of art is, Do you like it?

In general, this is an excellent criterion, but it's rather tricky. It has merit because in the end one likes a work of art or one doesn't, and that's all there is to it. There is no way to argue a preference based on personal taste—for example, choosing Mozart over Beethoven, or Picasso over Matisse. But this yardstick is sometimes unreliable, because it's the *lasting* impression that counts. In a famous statement Bernini observed, "When a painting by Baroccio, who used bright colors and gave agreeable looks to his figures, is seen for the first time, even by a

Collection, Museum of Modern Art, New York. Lillie P. Bliss Bequest

connoisseur, it will please him perhaps better than a painting by Michelangelo, which at first glance looks so rude and unpleasant that it makes you turn your eyes away from it. Nevertheless, while you are turning away and leaving the room, Michelangelo's painting seems to detain you and call you back, and after having examined it for a while you are forced to say: Ah! and yet it is fine. At length it charms you insensibly and so deeply that you are loath to depart. And every time you behold it again it will look finer and finer. The reverse happens with a work of Baroccio's . . ."

This is what the "test of time" ought to mean—not so much the time of generations or centuries (for these are remarkably susceptible to changing tastes), as the time actually spent by an individual experiencing a specific work. First impressions are by no means useless—the connoisseur of art depends a great deal on his first impression, as does the politician with people. But the untrained eye should be wary of superficial enticements and be willing to give the unappealing or demanding work both time and effort. Many enduring works of art have won acceptance only over years, even generations. One sort of Cubist picture (Plate 10), for instance, has an immediate charm of color, an ease of disposition and a more immediate intelligibility of form—all of which makes it superficially more attractive than another example of Cubist art (Plate 11), in which an apparently dull coloring, a complex and difficult organization or a state of tensions often throw up barriers to those unfamiliar with its system. With familiarity, however, the second work becomes ever richer and more resonant in its tone, color, execution. The forms divulge almost endless fascination in their internal relationships and their contribution to the over-all composition. In this case, the difficult work is the more enduring, even though the other retains its charm and subtlety.

Not to be omitted from any discussion of misconceptions is the vague but extraordinarily widespread assumption that art is a kind of embellishment of life. It is not art, but craft that embellishes. The truly

PLATE 11: Pablo Picasso, *Ma Jolie*, 1911–12. Oil on canvas, 39⅜″ x 25¾″

meaningful, truly authoritative art of any time embodies experiences as wide and as deep as those in any other sphere of human activity.

In an age that valued religion above all, Dante testified that art itself amounted to a religious experience. In our own age, which sees life in terms of history, Henri Focillon has not gone too far in saying that "a work of art rises proudly above any interpretation we may see fit to give it; and, although it serves to illustrate history, man, and the world itself, it goes further than this; it creates man, creates the world, and sets up within history an immutable order."

There are many other rampant misconceptions, and they plague critics of modern art as well as laymen. I have discussed those which seem to me the most virulent. To keep them in mind may help as we proceed to examine the main course of modern art from Impressionism to the present.

IV | MODERN MOVEMENTS IN ART

Perpetual modernness is the measure of merit in every work of art. —RALPH WALDO EMERSON

No man of sense can think that an imitation of the objects of nature is the art of painting. —WILLIAM BLAKE

Modern art did not begin with Impressionism. It began with the modern age, in that radical and violent last quarter of the eighteenth century (and some of the first examples of modern art appeared before the French Revolution). But the story of modern art from the time of Goya is too long for the scope of this book. Besides, there are certain good reasons for starting with Impressionism. For one thing, it was with the later forms of this style that the art of our century really began. For another, Impressionism was the first style that was really modern in outlook, without baggage or backward glance. Also, Impressionism is apparently the historical style with which the public of this generation is most completely at home. Ask the untutored layman to paint a picture, and he will very probably try his hand at a landscape or still life, and very probably with an impressionistic approach.

The most important reason for starting with Impressionism is rather complicated. Earlier art can be understood, to a high degree, by a simple if serious examination of its surroundings. That is, a statue on a Gothic cathedral becomes meaningful if one relates its content to contemporary theological values, and its style to that of the architecture on which it is placed. Or a painting of Raphael can be appreciated through comparison with contemporary philosophy and letters, and by examination of the spatial and figural organization. With modern art, however—to a considerable extent for the nineteenth century and still more so for the twentieth—an understanding of the nature of the art and an appreciation of its qualities depends on a familiarity with its historical development.

Why this is so is not important here; it is a fact of modern life. But it is not too much to say that art since Cézanne needs art history. To understand a given form of modern art requires a grasp of its place in a historical sequence. And because Cézanne cannot be understood without Impressionism, it is here that we must begin.

Certain perceptions which were revolutionary with the Impressionists are now a part of everyday visual experience. One can recognize this in a typical early Impressionist painting by Claude Monet (Color Plate 1). Foremost is the perception that the color of an object is not something which belongs to the object, but is rather a product of the ways in which sunlight and shadow and reflected light play upon it. To portray this phenomenon, Monet eliminated "earth colors"—black, brown, gray and tan—and used only the colors of the spectrum. The Impressionists perceived that true color is derived from sunlight, which can be broken down into the primary colors—red, yellow and blue—and their intermediary combinations. Thus, what appears to be an earth color is actually a spectral color at an uncharacteristic intensity (strength) and value (degree of light and dark). For example, "tan" is not "tan"—it is actually a yellow at low intensity. In earlier landscapes if a painter wanted to convey a tan, he usually mixed an earth color, which had the advantage of textural suggestion at the expense of optical accuracy.

Beginning with the Impressionists, the sensation of color was conveyed by "optical mixing" (as opposed to the earlier palette mixing). Observe the water in the Monet. It is not painted with a solid blue-green tone, as in earlier art, where the color of an area was predetermined and its equivalent in paint mixed upon the palette before being applied to the canvas. Instead, there is a large variety of separate hues, painted in brush strokes that lie close together but do not merge. The mixing is done by the eye at a certain distance; but if the eye is not too far away (arm's length is best), the colors begin to vibrate, providing both a greater intensity of color, seen as evocative of nature, and at the same time, an intensity of vibration, conveyed by the brush strokes themselves. The rhythm of the strokes is free and spontaneous, but they have a certain uniformity: in length, width and density, all the strokes are within a given range, and they curve slightly or form dashes (for this reason, Monet's is sometimes called the "comma" stroke).

From passage to passage the brush strokes seem to engage in a lyrical dance, making a sort of woven fabric across the surface of the picture, thereby providing unity and making the surface seem almost tangible. This is the first kind of painting in which the sensation of the individual brush strokes and of their agglomerative effect is thrust so immediately at the spectator that they become indispensable elements in the picture. (There are, however, important antecedents: Titian, Frans Hals, Constable and Delacroix, among others.)

Further, the brushwork activity is not confined to the area of an object, and neither is it subordinated to some preconceived order of composition, as in older painting. Instead, the strokes operate as a kind of open field. Like the scientific views of that time, such an approach presents an intuition of atomistic activity, with sensations of magnetic attractions and dispersals, or of chemical precipitations and suspensions.

The art in an Impressionist picture lies in the rhythms, notes, keys and harmonies of pure color; in the singing quality of its light; in the resonance, the veritable tangibility of its brushwork, which makes the canvas appear to be caressed. Few works in the entire history of art are as joyous, spontaneous and untroubled as these. Surely it is testimony to the stature and independence of art to recall that the most characteristic of these paintings were achieved in the years of France's military and political shame, and that individually the painters were not only denied any official recognition but were actually starving.

While this art can be appreciated for its "musical" qualities, these should not prevent us from seeing the life values asserted in Impressionism. Had these artists been of a didactic rather than empirical breed, they might very well have proclaimed the reputed last words of their English predecessor, Turner: "The sun is God." For if this art was not merely music, neither was it sheer visual experimentation.

The spectral palette was insisted upon for the transcription of color chiefly because this generation—and indeed, the nineteenth century in general (it was Delacroix who said, "Banish all earth colors")—identified life with energy and energy with the sun and its radiation. The light that pulsates in an Impressionist painting not only reveals a new way of observing the natural world; it is highly eloquent of a view of life. The light is conveyed in terms of pure color because that is the way the spectrum breaks down, but also for a strictly historical reason: Impressionism is the final stage, the Indian summer, of a tradition of rendering light and form in terms of color—a tradition that goes directly through Delacroix to Fragonard, Watteau, and on back to Rubens, Giorgione and Titian.

And "Indian summer" suggests another quality, related to the Impressionists' fascination with the sun—a certain persistent warmth. Since they worked out of doors and the year round, the Impressionists also painted dark skies, icy rivers and snow on the hills. But even these scenes appear gently warm by comparison with Turner's snowstorms at sea or the powerful mountain snowscapes of Courbet.

The true subject of the Impressionist picture is not the poppy field, or the sailing basin, or dancing on the green, but the sunlight itself: its vital condition and its role. Having observed the importance of this light as a theme, people sometimes say that the Impressionists chose motifs from nature indiscriminately, that they did not care *what* they saw, only how they saw it. To say this is to miss too much. Not even the most abstract painters are careless of the content of their art—of those particular areas of life that motivate their work.

All genuine artists are men who not only see but who care. It follows as the sun the shadow that the work of any artist will betray powerful and recurrent themes, aspects of life that have for him an ultimate meaning. So it was with the Impressionists—certain locales, certain motifs, certain sensations, recur again and again.

In still another sense the Impressionists were the first truly modern movement: instead of being scattered in town and country, they belonged to one of the new international cities. Their predecessors (Corot, Courbet, Turner) had worked from the Mediterranean to the North Sea, from Brittany to the Alps; even Constable had little to do with London, preferring to spend most of his life in one English county. But one cannot conceive of Impressionism without Paris. From then on, whether a painter lived and worked in the city or at a considerable distance from it, or even went to the South Seas, the center and the only center of his world, from aesthetic intercourse to the marketing of pictures, was Paris. And Paris was larger than France.

Since the Impressionists were above all involved with external nature, they did not necessarily paint in the city, though there is a surprising number of urban scenes—from boulevards to locomotive sheds. Monet and his fellows worked in the environs of Paris, up and down the Seine, in Montmartre (then a country town) and in the neighboring fields. They liked to paint boats, the ice and mist on a river, water lilies suspended in a pool, suburban lanes casually overhung with foliage, cheery houses viewed through a network of trees, the avenues of Paris with their chatty, chaotic commerce, spied from a window above; or falling snow, or apple blossoms, or the grasses, paths and fruit trees of an idle meadow in an eternal moment of sunlit peace.

Impressionism stands as the last truly easeful and happy painting. Henceforth, ease gave way to tension; joy to disturbance and agitation; peace to conflict; harmony to turmoil. In art, the twentieth century begins to take hold a little before 1890, with the later forms of Impressionism, with Post-Impressionism and Symbolism. This book will not deal with these movements as movements, but rather with certain key developments that mark the way, certain steps which must become familiar before the next can be understood.

In Impressionism the primary emphasis was still on the visual and tactile experience of natural phenomena, even though that emphasis was shifted from the object to the environment. As early as Edouard Manet's *Déjeuner sur l'Herbe* the figures and objects are dislocated so that the major theme becomes the atmosphere. All through Impressionism this is the case. Unique, vibrant, almost tangible, the atmosphere conditions the effects of the brush strokes. The dust, smoke, mist and moisture in the air infuse an atmosphere which unifies and interprets the objects and figures and in a sense becomes more real than they.

But when the Post-Impressionists sought to give a new pictorial structure to the apperceptions of Impressionism—to give it a sense of permanence, as with Paul Cézanne or Georges Seurat, or to charge it with emotion, as with Vincent van Gogh or Paul Gauguin—they had to dispense with this atmosphere. Not that their pictures lack a *sense* of atmosphere: like the Impressionists, the Post-Impressionists painted

Collection, Museum of Modern Art, New York. Gift of Madame Katia Granoff

PLATE 12: Claude Monet, Water Lilies, circa 1920. Oil on canvas, 51½″ x 79″

mostly from nature and in response to a particular motif. But the palpable atmosphere could no longer have freedom to exist as a substance, for that would be too momentary, too casual, too empirical; above all, it would interfere with new principles of rhythm and structure. Even in an "Impressionist" painting by Gauguin, a compulsion for rhythmic drawing overcomes that molecular structure of light and atmosphere which marked Monet.

The later Monet, while remaining an Impressionist, went far beyond the Impressionism of 1870. In the eighties and nineties he turned from his earlier, more comprehensive scenes to exercises in concentrated vision. Setting up his easel in the balcony of a hotel room opposite the façade of the cathedral at Rouen, he painted the incredibly complex interreflections of light in the street and on the façade of the cathedral at intervals during the day. These studies show a more severe disintegration of the object-in-light than Impressionism proper (late 1860's to late 1880's) ever contemplated. Further, they are best seen together, as studies reflecting each other.

The idea of reflections, which took place in nature in the early paintings (in scenes of rippled water or grass) has been extended so that the paintings reflect each other. One might also say that in going beyond the depiction of a scene simply for what it is, the later Monets can no longer be thought of as "pictures" (the earlier Impressionist paintings were the last "pictures" in art) and are more properly thought of as paintings.

Similar to the Rouen paintings were another series of reflecting works by Monet—this time of haystacks. In these paintings, color changes from the impressionistic to the expressionistic. Still later, in Venice and London, two of the wettest cities in Europe, Monet carried his explorations far beyond the pure surface reflections of the earlier millponds and quiet rivers by plunging so deeply into the waters and the mists that the one cannot always be distinguished from the other, and the spectator has no stationary location in the shifting landscape.

But it is above all in the water lilies of the pond in his own back yard that Monet produced works which lead directly from the Impressionism of 1870 to a kind of abstract impressionism virtually foretelling the state of painting in the mid-twentieth century. Plunging into these lily ponds, superficially the most ordinary of all his natural scenes, he developed something new and strange in pictorial experience, and virtually cosmic in its apprehension of space.

Many of these canvases are gigantic, and they are sometimes arranged so that the viewer is literally surrounded. Peering at the surface of a lily pond (Plate 12), one feels drawn into limitless depths, reflecting, back and forth, surfaces of all kinds, from the submarine bottom to the endless sky, with fluctuating layers of swimming and floating plant life. An intuition of space, not as the measurable interval between defined objects, but as something positive that develops by itself, and in so doing redefines all objects and forms, has been accomplished so effectively in these pictures (some of them painted in the 1920's), that not until thirty years later, in the work of Jackson Pollock, Sam Francis or Philip Guston, were further steps taken in this direction.

In the later Monet, as in Post-Impressionistic painting, the light, which in Impressionism proper had been derived objectively from the condition of nature, seems to be self-created. This is also true of the later works of Auguste Renoir.

By native temperament, Renoir was in conflict with the overwhelming instinct and direction of his time. In the Renaissance he would probably have devoted most of his attention to painting and sculpting the human figure. (Even in such an anti-sculptural age as the nineteenth century, he was responsible for some of the few significant pieces of sculpture.) But

Renoir emerged as an artist at the moment when Impressionism was realizing its style in landscape. Working beside Monet in the fields, he created some of the most stunning paintings of this school. But as the fifteen-year generation that marked the course of Impressionism's creative power came to an end, Renoir was suddenly confronted with his own preference for the human figure.

At first he sought to render the figure, especially the nude, in the sunbathed landscapes of Impressionism. But this led to a virtual contradiction in terms. We experience the figure—our own figure—in terms of weights, volumes and substances, articulated through motor activities and defined by absolute boundaries. These terms were precisely those inherent in Renaissance style, and it is no accident that in Renaissance painting and sculpture, the figure played its most important role since the ancient Greeks.

But such terms are antithetical to the primary experiences of Impressionism. For these experiences require external nature, seen through sunlight and shadow and especially in the kind of motif that is identified with Impressionism. While the Impressionists did paint still lifes, even portraits, their still lifes were largely indoor extensions of nature, and their portraits largely *tours de force*. Renoir, of all people, painted an Impressionist portrait of Wagner!

After an intense struggle between the human figure, which motivated his art, and the Impressionist approach, which was the mode he chose to work in, Renoir brilliantly resolved the two in his last years (Plate 13). This could not be accomplished through any real compromise between the sculpture-and-drawing kind of vision and the painting-Impressionist kind, but rather through the creation of an inner light in the painting that fused with the flesh and flowers and created a new texture. This inner light is not mystical; instead, it transfigures the substances of the external world and arrives at a new synthesis. This "self-created" light belongs generally to the twentieth century, and it also characterizes the work of such descendants of Renoir as Pierre Bonnard or Tony Vevers (Color Plate 9), not to mention Henri Matisse (Color Plate 4).

Though born a year earlier than Monet, two years before Renoir, and dead before either, Cézanne created an art form that belongs to a later generation. Reacting against the ephemeral quality of pure Impressionism (one of its chief charms) and against the casualness of its approach and the randomness of its composition, Cézanne sought, as he said, to make of Impressionism something solid, like the art in museums. By this he meant a more considered painting (though for all its happy spontaneity, a good Impressionist painting is much more considered than it looks), a more formally structured composition, a more systematic relationship between the total structure and the execution (i.e., brushwork).

Cézanne is famous for remarking that Monet (one of the few living painters whom he thoroughly admired) was "only an eye, but what an eye!" Ironically, it is Cézanne's visual perception that is not only one of

Collection, Museum of Modern Art, New York. Gift of Mr. and Mrs. Paul Rosenberg

PLATE 13: Auguste Renoir, *Reclining Nude*, 1902. Oil on canvas, 26½" x 60⅝"

the outstanding qualities of his art but also a fundamental element in his aesthetics. The fact is that Cézanne wound up doing more things at once, more important things, in a fully integrated and resolved style, than any other painter since Rembrandt—or to date, than any painter since himself. He had, as Matisse observed, so many things in mind at once that more than anyone else, he had to keep his mind in order.

This need for order produced a grand architecture of painting. In the sense of creating new, vital and organic structures, Cézanne might, by an extension of terminology, be called the greatest architect of his century; certainly few painters have been more concerned with structure.

Consider, for example, the *House in Provence*, now in the Herron Museum of Art in Indianapolis (Color Plate 2). Though less so than Monet, Cézanne's subject matter was still dominated by landscape. But unlike Monet, who preferred more mobile motifs, Cézanne inclined toward bare, firmly structured trees, clean-cut rock forms and a more frequent use of man-made architecture. It is the integration of these different elements—the organic, the geologic and the artificial—and their almost infinite interramifications, all conveyed in a conscious yet constantly probing and self-adjusting abstract design, that makes *House in Provence* so extraordinary.

Whereas in an Impressionist painting one would speak of the "motif" as a particular aura of sensations permeating a scene under certain conditions of nature, here the motif takes on a different significance: it might be described as an essay on the function of a building in a landscape. The essence of the building is expressed in vertical and horizontal lines, and these become the essential framework of the painting. The strongest vertical in the building—the left edge—is echoed by the farthest left edge of the mass of trees. This accent is picked up again in the strongest break in the mountain, where it begins its final decline. The viewer is provided with a fundamental axis in the picture—one which, however, is not picked up, as might be expected, at the other end of the house. To have done so would have been to cut the building out of its environment.

Instead, the far edge of the house is broken, first by an unexplained, shedlike extension; then by a tree which seems to coincide with the edge but splits into several vertical branches at angles to it. One of these branches runs parallel to the edge of the house, and at the top, joins the line running down from the roof. This ties in the foreground tree, the middle-ground house and the vegetation behind, producing a tensely solid shape, negative in terms of the objects and space of the picture, but positive in its captivating character.

The same thing happens with the long horizontal patches just in front of and behind the house. Though these must be read as empty fields, their role in the picture is unmistakably related to the two long horizontal sweeps of solid rock that dominate the top of the picture. Besides tying in top and bottom, they also relate left and right, for both in their linear pitch and color tone, as they develop at the right, they correspond to the pitch and tone of the rooftop.

The more distant field is a continuation of the lines and shapes at the end of the house. The closer field reaches all the way to the left in a long horizontal which replaces the base of the house; yet this in turn is concealed by changing but continuous forms of vegetation. The effect is to anchor the house more firmly than if it rested only on its own foundations; at the same time, the vegetation, like the fields, ties the house into the surrounding landscape, so that instead of sticking out blocklike and man-made, it is incorporated into the scheme of nature.

This process is carried out in many other respects. While the bottom of the roof is a straight horizontal—echoing the straightness of the bottom of the foreground patch, and by implication, the firm base of the painting itself—the top of the roof is a convex curve. This pulls the house into an inexorable tension with the top edge of the lower mountain range and also with a rooflike form that projects from the mountain. This part-angular, part-convex quality is picked up on the left side of the higher mountain range, but its right side is horizontal, and so both anchors the top edge of the painting and echoes the straightest part of the foreground shape, which is at the lower left.

The foreground tree, in addition to helping tie the house into its setting, also makes it part of the series of flat planes that are basic to the architecture of the painting. These planes emphasize the flat surface of the painting, just as the verticals and horizontals emphasize the shape and the dimensions. All of this reflects a reiterated consciousness of a painting as something executed on a flat surface of a chosen size, shape and disposition. The surface is emphasized as important in itself. Similarly, it emphasizes the architecture *of* the picture as superseding the architecture *in* the picture—that is, the structure of the house.

Just as the house is prevented from popping out of the picture by the rearrangement and obliteration of its potentially boxlike appearance, so the elements of the house are made more visually interesting by various arbitrary devices. None of the windows are related "properly"—to one another, to the door or even to the edges of the building. Thus, instead of being absorbed into a preconceived order, each develops its own individual character, its own validity as a shape. The pictorial relation of each to the other is established through qualities persistent in the characterization, providing an order that is organic as opposed to the more mechanical order in a system of strict perspective. For example, the shape and near axis of the door is related to the window nearest above it, a window which is "pointed to" by the branches of two trees, one on either side of the door.

The chimney is the pictorial focal point of the whole painting. In a vertical direction it relates the emphatic bare tree at center foreground with the tallest, most central of the background trees, which are all in foliage; this latter tree is a direct continuation of the chimney and might almost seem to grow out of it except that such a possibility is countered by the continuation of the roof line, which runs jaggedly across the top of the chimney and off into a patch of much more distant foliage, which in turn takes on characteristics of both the rocks above and the fields below. The right edge of the chimney runs back down along the edge of the roof and ties into the tree with which this discussion began. The gridwork set up in and around this chimney extends ultimately, in one form or another, to all parts and aspects of the painting. As a result, the whole picture has a centrifugal energy and an electrifying tension in sharp contrast to the centripetal piling up that was characteristic of composition in the Renaissance.

Yet this dispersion detracts nothing from the extraordinary solidity and compactness of the entire painting, qualities symbolized in the structure of the house itself. The "theme" of centrifugal energy versus static form is continued, with variation, in the theme of open and closed forms. At first glance, it appears that the closed forms are gathered in the left half of the painting, the open ones in the right. The left has the house, the foliate trees and the more solid rocks; the right half leans to open fields, bare trees with spreading branches and two-dimensional rock formations.

But look again at the trees. The bare ones project their branches in eloquent arm gestures that make them stronger visually than the more amorphous, patch-painted foliate trees. The house is rendered as a dense, solid object; yet the larger surfaces are surprisingly light, and the left end of the house is painted in a mysterious openness which renders it almost concave; the branches of a foliate tree nearby are spread so widely that the tree is overcome and displaced by the bands of fields supposedly behind it. Above that a bright patch of hilltop continues by implication the shadow of the roof on the other end of the house, and this again contributes to opening the house into the landscape.

The major elements of the painting, then, while self-distinct, as befits the classical mood of Mediterranean art, are visually interrelated. The

most organic elements—the foliate trees—are focused on the least organic—the man-made house. To a certain extent these two extremes
immobilize one another, and the most dynamic activity is in the semi-
static, semiorganic forms of bare trees, bare fields and bare rocks.

Cézanne had said, "To paint a landscape properly, I must first discover the geological basis." And all the arbitrary pictorial orchestration
in a painting such as *House in Provence* should not make one blind to
the profound intuition of both the form and the growth of rock and hill,
and out of them, tree and meadow. In the South of France, just as in
Italy, the hand of man working on and in the landscape over thousands
of years has produced an architecture of nature, within which ordered
form and free growth are constantly interactive.

At the same time that the evidence of man's hand is found throughout the landscape, his buildings not only correspond to it, but as they
age, begin to settle and partially crumble into field and hill. It is just
such buildings that Cézanne frequently sought out: buildings like this
house, or the *Château Noir*, or the *House with Cracked Walls*, or the
House of the Hanged Man. With a comparable interest he often turned
to the quarry at Bibemus, the blocks and millstones in the woods, the
broken trees and rocks at Fontainebleau, and the hilltop towns.

Pierre Bonnard incisively described Cézanne's approach to nature and
to his art: "Cézanne in front of the subject had a firm idea of what he
wanted to do, and only took from nature that which reaffirmed his
concept. He often just went there to rest—to be the lizard—to heat
himself in the sun without ever touching a brush. He could wait
until the things became what they were in his conception. He was the
painter most powerfully armed before nature, the purest, the most
sincere."

Much of the magic of Cézanne's art lies in this integration of the
abstract orderings envisioned by his mind with the touching passion of

fluid life. As an artist he has been claimed to be now classical, now gothic —the secret being that he is both at once, to a degree almost unique in Western painting.

In contrast, Van Gogh is utterly gothic. Where Cézanne turned the excitements and techniques of Impressionism into orchestrations of form, Van Gogh transformed them into instruments of passion, which he proceeded to orchestrate in quite a different way.

In Van Gogh's portrait of Dr. Gachet, although the setting is evidently the interior of a room, the background is painted in broad sweeps of light and dark blue. What sense does this make? Two years earlier, Van Gogh had written to his brother Théo about an idea for an earlier portrait. He describes the tenor of such a picture and then writes: "But the picture is not finished yet. To finish it I am now going to be the arbitrary colorist. I exaggerate the fairness of the hair, I come even to orange tones, chromes, and pale lemon yellow.

"Beyond the head, instead of painting the ordinary wall of the mean room, I paint infinity, a plain background of the richest, intensest blue that I can contrive, and by this simple combination of the bright head against the rich blue background, I get a mysterious effect, like a star in the depths of an azure sky."

What happens in the Gachet portrait is significant in several ways. One is the "mysterious effect" that Van Gogh anticipated, and this is part of the reason one can call him an artist in the gothic vein—that and his transcendence of the "ordinary wall of the mean room." Another result is, as the art historian Oskar Hagen once put it, that there is an "imperturbably superior blue that resounds through this whole picture: something of the superior personality of the physician is in it."

Still another significance lies in the analogy to the "depths of an azure sky." Like Cézanne and Monet and most of their generation, Van Gogh was above all a nature painter. As Renoir transformed flesh and figure into new substances sympathetic with nature, so Van Gogh translated much of his passion for humanity into the very forms of nature. The humanity resonant in a Rembrandt painting, evoked in the shadows of a dusty room, is echoed by Van Gogh "in the depths" of the natural universe. For him any other realm would have been inadequate.

By the same token, as Rembrandt found his fullest and richest subjects in portraiture (though he was a great landscape artist), so Van Gogh (though he was a great portraitist) found his most compelling themes in nature. Consider the background of *The Starry Night* (Plate 24). Not only is it a deep blue, extraordinary in its inner emotion, but it runs in waves. This overwhelmingly rhythmic quality forces itself into every corner of his mature painting, surging with a passion unseen since the old German woodcuts and producing a glow of color, an inner radiance of light and a luminescence of paint that not only transforms all nature into a sublime nerve storm, but pushes painting virtually beyond its own limits.

These rhythmic qualities are carried from the smallest touch of the brush to the vast crescendo that sweeps through the entire composition and is comparable to the development of a symphony. More than Manet, Whistler or Gauguin, all of whom thought more consciously about the relationship of the two arts, Van Gogh pulls painting from its own realm into that of music. And yet his painting remains very much an art realized in pictorial terms. Of that generation only Cézanne equals Van Gogh in his integration of meaning with style. Compared to these two giants, Gauguin is all too often flat or empty. In a superb reservation (reminding us that in the end it is usually artists who are the most trenchant critics), Edvard Munch remarked: "Ah, he [Van Gogh] was a really great man. And Gauguin too. One always recognizes him. But isn't he a little bit too general at times?"

.   .   .

If Van Gogh's art is both music and motif, it is also painting: mountains and valleys of paint, applied furiously yet with an intense control of the thick, gleaming impastos, with their incomparable luster—paint so thick that some of it is not yet dry, luminous both because of its response to nature and because of a light that can only be called self-created.

But Van Gogh is not only painter and musician; he is also poet. His pictures, whether of man or nature, are incomprehensible without their motivation to communicate experience and give it a name. This desire to communicate is revealed in one of his own letters: ". . . the study of color. I am always in hope of making a discovery there, to express the love of two lovers by a marriage of two complementary colors, their mingling and their opposition, the mysterious vibrations of kindred tones. To express the thought of a brow by the radiance of a light tone against a somber background." Here is expressionism—and more.

"To express hope by some star, the eagerness of a soul by a sunset radiance. Certainly there is nothing in that of stereoscopic realism, but is it not something that actually exists?"

Van Gogh's poetic urge to "name" is evident, I think, in a simple portrait of a chair. Here is a prime example of the pathetic fallacy in art. The chair becomes an object inseparable from human life and value and is itself more "human" than the most vivid figure by a lesser artist.

Van Gogh is also entitled to consideration as a poet on the basis of what he wrote. While this consists almost entirely of private letters unintended for publication, the literary value has been proclaimed by critics and poets alike. These letters reveal the quality which is keenest of all in Van Gogh's painting: the strongest emotions developed to an abnormally pure pitch. In comparison to the spontaneity and gallant cheerfulness of the Impressionists, Van Gogh inundates nature and man in waves of anguish and pity, exaltation and joy. Out of tragic depths emerges a beauty that passes definition.

. . .

Wider in his experience of life than Cézanne, Van Gogh was narrower as an artist. Still, in drawing, coloring, painting and composing, Van Gogh was one of the supreme modern artists, and in sacrifice and commitment, second to none. Here lies much of his importance to Expressionists and Abstract Expressionists alike—two of the most important of twentieth-century traditions. Van Gogh's art seems to flow in one irrevocable direction. Though statistically the most popular (not long ago it was determined that more reproductions of Van Goghs were sold than of any other artist), his art is lonely, and few artists have been able to take from it directly.

Nearly the opposite is true of Cézanne. His art, discreetly divorced from life's immediate entanglements, was the most comprehensive since Rubens and the most influential at least since Delacroix. What Cézanne actually achieved in his style is still more extraordinary. From an originally heavy, almost clumsy hand and impatient spirit, he forged the most titanic system of drawing fused with painting since Titian, who perhaps alone is comparable to Cézanne in molding a style in which drawing and painting are absolutely inseparable. Delacroix spent his whole career in such an attempt and almost succeeded; he is the immediate link between Titian and Cézanne. Even Rembrandt, whose drawing and painting are without peer in Western art, did not seek to merge drawing and painting in such an interdependence.

Color and light, stroke and passage, edge and area, position and movement, are all interactive and interdependent in Cézanne. One cannot apprehend space without color, color without light, light without form, form without space. This is why Cézanne could spend an entire day putting in one or two strokes—and then very possibly take them out again. Sometimes this meant that parts of the canvas were left bare, but it would be dangerous to conclude that these are unfinished paintings;

the phenomenon is too frequent and too consistent (as with Michelangelo's late "unfinished" sculpture). Moreover, the bare canvas plays a role in this new sense of painting, calling attention to the surface as an aesthetic factor.

So deft and articulate was Cézanne's developed aesthetic, so well integrated were his smallest touch and his total style, that innumerable followers mistook the outward manner for the method, and whole careers during the following generation were sunk under the weight of Cézanne's style. Such a disaster is equaled only by the example of Giotto in the early fourteenth century. In both cases the major spirits survived, and they benefited enormously; Matisse, Picasso and Braque were large enough to absorb Cézanne in some significant way and then proceed on their own.

Less devastating but still of major significance was the all too brief career of Georges Seurat. More scientific in temperament than most artists, Seurat developed formulas critical to the aesthetics of modern painting. Though his art suffered to some extent from overapplication, even his most theoretical pictures are poetic as well as eloquent in their style and aesthetic concept.

Le Chahut (Plate 14), in the Albright Gallery in Buffalo, exemplifies key aspects of Seurat's technique and composition. Technically, the freer, more spontaneous and temperamental brush stroke of the Impressionists is replaced by that of the Neo-Impressionists (as Seurat, Paul Signac and others called themselves). This new brush stroke consisted of small dots and dashes, carefully measured and deliberately located—a technique which is sometimes called "pointillism." The purpose of the Neo-Impressionists was to combat the earlier effect of a momentary sensation, as well as any suggestion of whimsy or accident. In addition, the dot would help prevent the overlapping of strokes. Anything that looks like a line or an edge is discovered on closer examination to be actually a series of dots, or "points" of color. So the atomism of Impressionism is carried considerably further.

On the other hand, the apparent haphazardness of an Impressionist composition—by which a picture appeared to be far more casually structured than it actually was—is replaced by a high degree of calculation; less instinctive than Van Gogh's, less empirical than Cézanne's, such compositions are virtually products of the laboratory.

Here are some of Seurat's rules, and they can be applied without further comment to *Le Chahut*. I shall not describe the colors; they ought to describe themselves. Seurat prescribed:

"Gaiety of tone is given by the dominance of light; of color, by the dominance of warm colors; of line, by the dominance of lines above the horizontal [i.e., upward].

"Calm of tone is given by an equivalence of light and dark; of color, by an equivalence of warm and cold; and of line, by horizontals.

"Sadness of tone is given by the dominance of dark; of color, by the dominance of cold tones; and of line, by downward directions."

There is nothing radically new in these concepts; since the beginning of art, painters have instinctively made such choices to convey the mood of their subject. What *is* new is that the aesthetic concepts themselves become the subject of the painting, and the figures merely instruments. In Renaissance art it was the other way around. From the Neo-Impressionists' experiments in color, light, accent and form, it is but a step to much of what goes on in the twentieth century's more abstract painting.

Significant too is Seurat's painting of the picture frame. Considering the frame not as something that separates the picture from its surroundings and is therefore equally set off from the picture itself, Seurat developed a frame which extended the picture into its environment. For this reason he painted his own frames, using the same technique as in

PLATE 14: Georges Seurat, *Study for Le Chahut*, 1889. Oil on canvas, 22″ x 18¼″

the paintings, with each part of the frame responding to whatever it bordered. With Latin logic, however, he still sought to distinguish the two, saying that "the frame is in a harmony contrasted to that of the tones, the colors, and the lines of the picture." The frame thus becomes a sort of middle ground between the painting and its actual environment.

In the twentieth century, artists have become more and more interested in the possibilities of a painting to expand, both in its inner workings and its physical existence. Some, like John Marin, have pursued Seurat's practice of rendering the frame a part of or a continuation of the picture; some have used a floating frame; others have settled for the simple strip, barely visible, that holds the canvas on the edge of the stretcher. Still others have eschewed even the strip and let the painting continue over the edge, thus not only projecting the painting further into nature, but emphasizing that the work is complete in itself and that a frame would be extraneous.

Neither these practices nor Seurat's explain anything about the art itself; that remains a matter of individual genius. With some of Seurat's work, one feels that either the composing or the transcription of light effects (especially when he worked by oil lamp at night, mathematically calculating its differences from sunlight) is so methodical that the picture is a bit dry; other of his pictures, done more directly from nature, are fresher. This has become a problem for the abstract artist as well; formula alone will produce nothing but procedure. Seurat once wrote, "They see poetry in what I have done. No, I apply my method, and that is all there is to it."

Strangely, that is *not* all there is to it. For one thing, it is the poetry and nothing else that makes Seurat a real artist. But all poetry must be powerfully motivated; it does not just sing like the bird, in spite of what Picasso once said. And so in the end the poetry in Seurat's best paintings cannot be separated from that obsession with intellectualization and measurement—an obsession that was part of Seurat's native genius.

In Mondrian too (as we shall see) the poetry and the mechanics are inseparable, as is not the case with some of his followers, whose work can never be anything but good or bad examples of exercises after the fact. Mondrian himself was grievously aware of this and spoke words that should be a warning to all young artists: "What is wrong with the abstract painting of the younger artists today is that they feel their painting can begin where mine leaves off, without going through what mine has gone through to be the way it is."

V | CUBIST, BUT NOT ABSTRACT

There is [in Picasso] never any suspicion of conventional beauty.
—KANDINSKY

When we invented Cubism we had no intention whatever of inventing Cubism. —PICASSO

The two most significant and influential developments in twentieth-century art have been Cubism and Abstract Expressionism, and there is more relation between the two than is sometimes supposed. But whereas Abstract Expressionism, though awkward, is a good descriptive name, the term Cubism, though concise, could be very misleading.

Cubism does not deal in cubes. The only forms even resembling cubes are to be found in a few early, or proto-Cubist, pictures, such as Braque's *Road Near L'Estaque* of 1908 (Plate 15), or in some of the more mechanical work of such artists as Francis Picabia or Fernand Léger.

Consider Picasso's *Ma Jolie* (Plate 11) of 1911 and 1912, the key years of Cubism. Although *Ma Jolie* is composed essentially of highly formal elements, with a great many angular and some rectangular shapes, no shape ever becomes a finished object, such as a cube. Cubes

PLATE 15: Georges Braque, *Road near L'Estaque*, 1908. Oil on canvas, 23¾" x 19¾"

are to be found in Raphael or in Dürer—but theirs was an age that experienced the world in terms of objects, their location and definition. Our own age tends to view the world as varying fields of activity, which is also a good way to look at Cubist paintings.

The stage had been set for Cubism in certain aspects of the later work of Cézanne. From Cézanne to the Braque to *Ma Jolie* now appears to be a logical sequence of short steps. But the leap is wider than it looks.

Compare the Cézanne with the Picasso. Both reveal an architectonic structure. Both are highly interested in geometric relationships, squares, rectangles, triangles, arcs of circles. In neither picture, however, are such forms permitted to complete themselves; if they did, they would acquire an anti-modern quality of containment (remember that even Mondrian's forms are ordinarily not contained within the picture; they are cut off incomplete at the borders). Both paintings are concerned with the relationships between the brush strokes, the intermediary forms and the composition as a whole.

But in the Cézanne the abstract play of the lines and shapes is generally subordinated to the forms of architecture or of nature. Occasionally a line will break loose on its own and become an abstract mark, as in some of the center passages. Such passages create a splendid tension with the predominating lines, which outline the objects but delineate them in such a manner that the various lines, edges and angles change their roles back and forth from abstraction to representation. In the Picasso the situation is reversed. Whatever sense of life we have is a *result* of the abstract play of lines and shapes. In the Cézanne, although there may be tension between adjacent planes, there is very little of Picasso's ambiguity.

Ma Jolie is constructed on ambiguity. A plane which seems to be in front of its neighbor at one point will appear to be behind at another. In some areas the lines begin to vibrate as their roles change. A line that in one context works as an edge will change into a direction, next a support, then an axis, and perhaps a pure mark. But the line itself is not a real line, since it is almost always composed of a slightly irregular series of brush strokes, which in their directed order epitomize the principles that underlie the entire painting.

Before examining this painting further, it would be useful to observe more particularly how painting got to this stage. One step from the Cézanne may be seen in the Braque, where the architectural forms found in nature provided the basis for a geometrical composition. Though this is not the only route to Cubism, it is probably the most significant.

Another route is evident in Picasso's *Desmoiselles d'Avignon* (Color Plate 3), of 1907–8. Painted over a period of about a year, this picture is unusual in the history of art because stylistic decisions and developments are actually visible within it.

Evidently the two figures at center were painted first, then the figure at left, finally the two at the right. The two at center already begin to show a loss of female characteristics. Woman's hair, her crowning glory, has been partly removed from one and is almost entirely missing from the other. The roundness associated with woman is still dominant, but it is not pervasive, and sharp angles occur at a waist, an elbow, even a breast. The eyes are slightly differentiated, and the focus of the expression is further disturbed by the fact that the noses are in profile.

The figure at left marks a considerable breakaway, however, from the still cohesive femininity of the first two figures. The face is darkened now, in striking contrast to the body, further dehumanizing it. The left arm is related to the head pictorially rather than in terms of the figure; in feeling, color and shape it belongs to the same passage as the head, but anatomically it is almost impossible to explain. The body itself changes color; from the ivory cream of the first two figures, it turns to tones more suggestive of clay than of flesh, and around the outline of the left leg introduces a brilliant blue that complements the clay color. This leg, a

wonderfully rhythmic piece of drawing, defeminizes the figure still further by exaggerating the kneecap and enlarging the foot. But it is the
right leg and side of the woman on the left that do most to transform
her figure. The stiffness of the arm dispels any dulcet feminine effect; it
is a "dishpan" hand, or perhaps fist, and it immobilizes the left side of
the painting. The hip and leg are so fragmented that one can barely
distinguish solids from voids, although there are sensations of action in
the abstract movement of knee and heel.

The rendering gets increasingly abstract, moving left from the center
of the painting. The abstraction of the leg works into the brown area at
far left which might be read as abstract, empty space—or as a cave, or
still again as a curtain echoing a blue and white curtain on the right.
Possibly this was part of the original conception, which was to portray
the damsels of a house in Avignon Street in Barcelona. That the original
conception included a sailor and a figure bearing a warning skull as a
memento mori shows how far Picasso proceeded, within this picture
alone, from a literary to an abstract form of art.

As the picture developed, especially in the right half, this interchange-
ability of figure and ground became more prominent. Frequently a
"figure" passage is adjacent to a background passage that dominates it.
The effect is of painted planes interwoven across the entire picture
surface. At the same time, the deadening of the figures is countered by
the enlivening of action and gesture, and by an energetic handling of
paint in the "empty" areas.

On examining the two figures at right, one finds them less approach-
able. No longer merely disarrangement and discoloration, but now
real violence, has been done to face and figure. The face at the top is
robbed of vision and identity by blackening out the eye and is slashed
with streaks of bright green and red which extend into the beautiful
areas around the head, forbidding it to be isolated. One breast disap-

COLOR PLATE 1, above: Claude Monet, *Basin at Argenteuil, circa* 1874. Oil on
canvas, 22" x 29½"

COLOR PLATE 2, below: Paul Cézanne, *House in Provence*, 1885–86. Oil on canvas,
25¾" x 32"

Museum of Art, Rhode Island School of Design, Providence

Herron School of Art, Indianapolis

Collection, Museum of Modern Art, New York.
Acquired through Lillie P. Bliss Bequest

COLOR PLATE 3: Pablo Picasso, Les Desmoiselles d'Avignon, 1907.
Oil on canvas, 8′ x 7′8″

Collection, Museum of Modern Art, New York. Gift of Mr. and Mrs. Samuel A. Marx

COLOR PLATE 4: Henri Matisse, The Moroccans, 1916. Oil on canvas, 71⅜″ x 9′2″

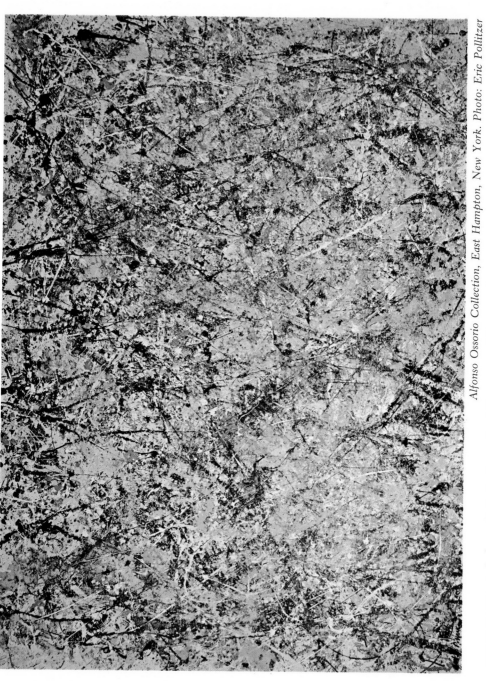

COLOR PLATE 5: Jackson Pollock, *Lavender Mist*, 1950. Oil, enamel and aluminum paint on canvas, 88" x 9'11"

COLOR PLATE 6: Giorgio Cavallon, 6-6-60, 1960. Oil on canvas, 48" x 76"   *Courtesy of The Singer Company, New York*

Collection of the Artist. Photo: Charles Uht

COLOR PLATE 7: Fritz Bultman, *Good News*, 1963. Oil on canvas, two panels, 8′x8′

8. John Ferren. No. 14 West. 1964. Oil on canvas, 65" x 80".

I.M. Pei Collection

Malcolm K. Fleschner Collection, Photo: Geoffrey Clements

COLOR PLATE 9: Tony Vevers, Cornfield, 1965. Oil on canvas, 44″ x 58″

Collection of the Artist

COLOR PLATE 10: Elizabeth Holliday, On the Grass III, 1965. Oil on canvas, 84″ x 96″

COLOR PLATE 11. Franz Kline, Scudera, 1961. Oil on canvas, 9′2½″ x 78″

pears into the shadow of an arm; the other becomes a diamond shape tacked onto the chin.

The figure at lower right is stylistically the most interesting. A kind of fishbone breaks up her forehead, the area suggestive of cerebration. The focus of expression is broken by the differentiation of the eyes: one runs into the brow, the other does not; one is oval, the other almond-shaped; one is white, one is blue; and they are at different angles. The great nose, like a piece of architecture—it resembles a bridge—cuts the face in two and pulls the mouth to one side. Nose and mouth have divided the face as much left and right as up and down.

The head is cupped in an enormous hand, of compelling shape. The shape is echoed in the wrist and arm, still again in thigh and buttock, and finds its final resting place in the great red slice of melon at the bottom. This is part of a still-life passage which is not only the strongest single passage in the painting, but is the culmination of the composition.

And that fact may be taken as prophetic. For still life was to become the prime subject matter of Cubism. Here the subject matter—fruit, organic nature—is still of a kind more readily associated with Impressionism and Post-Impressionism. In mature Cubism the still-life is dominated by artifacts, by objects with regularized, mathematically analyzable forms. Still life of this sort was to be as crucial to Cubism as landscape, in its chosen qualities, had been to Impressionism.

In Les Desmoiselles one can find an early example of the influence of African sculpture, which Picasso, Matisse, Amedeo Modigliani and other artists had discovered as a major art form early in the twentieth century. This influence is evident in the two heads at the right and probably in the one at far left. Picasso has denied any such influence at this time, but he is an old hand at trying to confuse art historians— possibly in order to give them something to do.

Also evident is the relationship of the passionately schematized heads and figures, especially the eyes, to ancient Iberian sculpture, a part of Picasso's heritage. Whereas the nineteenth century had referred, much more freely than before, to far-flung examples of late Gothic, Renaissance and Baroque art, and a little of the Far East, the twentieth century began in earnest to plumb the early Gothic, Romanesque and pre-Romanesque arts of the West (nineteenth-century artists had seldom ventured beyond the Greek and Roman, though Gauguin and Seurat were interested in the Egyptian), and in addition the arts of Africa, India or the South Pacific, which were often highly sophisticated as well as primitive.

Quite different from these sources, however, and very much in the tradition of Cézanne, is the sense of *struggle* in the Picasso. This is frequently a quality, and still more often a condition, of twentieth-century art. In a good picture the struggle must be resolved aesthetically; that is, the problems raised in the painting must be solved in terms of aesthetic satisfaction, as in *Les Desmoiselles*. But the sense of struggle—as an emotional condition—may remain.

The effect of this struggle may be fragmentation, as here in the human figure, a state of tension or a centrifugal tendency such as that to which Yeats referred ("Things fall apart; the centre cannot hold . . ."). Often in twentieth-century art, there is a wrenching of former meanings and values or an intentional ambiguity of relationships.

What is the meaning of this fragmentation and ambiguity? Many art historians, especially those less sympathetic to modern art, hold that such qualities are merely a reflection of the basic conditions of twentieth-century life, an era of wars and social dislocations almost without parallel.

Disregarding the issue of whether art is the flower of civilization or is rather, as Docteur Véron said, its germination, there is another way to approach this situation. All the qualities mentioned above proceeded steadily out of certain aspects of Impressionism—of the late Monet, of Cézanne and Van Gogh. Hence, they appear to be part of a progression containing an inner logic, and this same logic has given shape to our own pictures of the modern world: pictures with metaphysical, psychological and scientific dimensions.

That "the centre cannot hold" is only another way of indicating the need for expansiveness in twentieth-century life. (Henry Miller once wrote of a midwestern city that he could walk the entire main street and never meet an expansive soul.) The "fragmentation" can be interpreted as the necessary destruction of the old static object world, to be replaced by a new world realized primarily as a field of forces. And the wrenching, the ambiguity, can be seen as an awareness—whether in depth psychology, international politics or astrophysics—that one must always be ready to think the "unthinkable thought," to see oneself and the world from totally unexpected angles.

As much as any other activity, art forces a man specifically to see himself and his world. And so the relation between modern art and society has a positive side that in the end seems far more significant than its negative, which is the one usually talked about: the reflection of chaos and dislocation.

But the fact that for at least a century before Cubism, art had been evolving steadily toward these conditions suggests another way of accounting for them—in terms of the inner history of art itself. Like a political institution, an art form is a product not only of its relations with other forms of life, but of its own instinctual process of growth and development. There is an inner history of the United States Congress, as well as an outer one; that is, interior forces as well as exterior are responsible for its changing state. And there is a history of Impressionism (from around 1830 to around 1930) which can be understood *only in its own terms.*

In understanding these terms, one becomes aware of patterns which are rhythmic and to some extent cyclical. There is a noticeable rhythm in recent centuries of Western art history, according to which certain centuries are strikingly like others. The thirteenth century, for example, is very like the seventeenth in its over-all unity, ease, articulateness and comprehensibility of style. The fifteenth is like the nineteenth: both take a new, fresh, empirical, and wide-eyed look at the world of external nature.

And the twentieth century is astoundingly like the sixteenth. Both are periods of stylistic chaos; both follow upon a classical, sure summit of art (the High Renaissance in one case, Post-Impressionism in the other). Both are full of tensions, ambiguities, self-reflections, nervous energy, vast and often unrealizable ambitions, discontinuities and cul-de-sacs. These two centuries—more than any others—produced an art that was built on art.

All of these qualities suggest what has come to be called mannerism. This thought is a subject in itself; suffice it to say that much of the art of the sixteenth century was mannerist in one way or another, from the late Leonardo to the late Tintoretto, and that it will greatly help our apprehension of twentieth-century art to see in how many ways it too is a mannerist period. Cubism, Expressionism, Dada, Surrealism, Futurism, Magic Realism, Abstract Expressionism, Pop art—all have mannerist aspects. By the same token, there was a very real and literal cubism, a surrealism and an expressionism in the sixteenth century.

Part of what one sees in Picasso's *Les Desmoiselles* can only be understood by considering it historically. Even though it was not publicly exhibited until thirty years after it was painted, *Les Desmoiselles* had probably the largest influence on painters of any work of its time. This testifies in part to its revolutionary character, but the effect it created was too strong to depend entirely on novelty or shock.

Still, in terms of style *Les Desmoiselles* is not entirely resolved.

Strongly integrated pictorially, it nonetheless contains elements of several styles distant in both time and space.

For a painting in a resolved style, one must turn to *Ma Jolie*. Only in such a picture is it possible to find all the aspects of a Cubist painting. The strong colors that were at war with one another in *Les Desmoiselles* have been reduced to an almost monochromatic range of dull greens, grays and tans. Color has been subordinated to other elements, but it still plays a genuine role, for much of the spatial vibration as well as the mood are dependent on it. What color and light *per se* were to Impressionism, line and shape were to Cubism. Renoir had written a manifesto in 1884, "On the Importance of Irregularity in the Arts"; Georges Braque in 1917 said simply, "I like the rule that corrects the emotion."

Cubism is flatly opposed historically by its predecessor Impressionism, and geographically by its contemporary Expressionism. To suggest that Cubism is an art of rules is not to say that it proceeds according to rules; almost no modern style does that. But it is involved in ordering what it depicts, in giving to sensations a sense of ordered mutual relationships and a sense of measurement. For the rule both "corrects"—i.e., regulates—and seeks to measure objects in relation to each other.

That which is regulated and measured is no longer the simulated object or figure, as in older art, but rather the results of the rearrangement—even the destruction of that object or figure. In *Ma Jolie* the artist started with the figure of a woman playing a guitar. By the time he had finished, it was barely possible to make this subject out, and it is not entirely clear whether he meant her to be recognizable as a woman. That very lack of clarity is a part of the intentional ambiguity which is also evident in the spatial structure.

Out of the fragmentation of figure and object in Cubism emerges an entirely new set of forms, planes, areas and edges. This many-faceted structure is now subject to its own laws of order and development, maintaining, however, as mentioned earlier, certain persistent characteristics. These appear in the spatial organization, in the use of line and brush stroke and in the penchant for nearly geometric forms. Consider the frequency of triangles (or *near*-triangles, for none of these shapes is complete), especially long ones; they are all proportioned to the shape of the picture, as are the rectangles and near-rectangles and arcs of circles. Each of these forms is among the most easily grasped, most regulated, of conceivable shapes or accents.

But if one stresses the development of Cubism in terms of the "rule that corrects the emotion," it should not be forgotten that emotion remains. With Cubism the emotions are related to a significant and consistent subject matter. For example, printed words or letters appear and reappear. "Ma Jolie" was the title of a popular song, and the words are a part of the picture, looking much like the printing on the top of a song sheet. The other two significant elements in *Ma Jolie* that have been mentioned so far—the single human figure and the musical instrument—are also recurrent subjects. Typically too, here and in a good many other Cubist works there are such elements as cigarettes and pipes, bottles and glasses, books and newspapers, tabletops and musical notations. The musical instrument appears frequently, and it is usually of a certain kind: guitar, violin, mandolin, banjo or clarinet. These are instruments that belong not to the symphony orchestra or even the chamber group but to the individual secluded in his study. Among the parts of the human figure that count most are the forehead, nose and eyes, the elbows, hands and fingers.

Taking all these factors together, what aspects of life are expressed in Cubist painting? Clearly it is an indoor life—domestic, yet not of the kitchen (as in Dutch seventeenth-century painting), nor of the boudoir (as in French eighteenth-century painting), nor of the sitting room (as in English eighteenth-century painting). Instead, it centers in the private study, that last stronghold of an older and highly refined culture which was largely wiped out with the First War. Our idea of a study today is usually little more than a male hideaway in homes dominated by women and children. The study echoed in Cubist art was a world unto itself, an environment created for himself by the Old World Parisian. Here his character, values and interests were reflected in every object. The books were not for show—they were his favorites; and they covered a range of tastes unusual today. The pipes and cigarettes, wines and brandies were a matter of experienced choice; the paintings and the sculptures (which, in this last residue of the Renaissance, included small casts and bronzes which could be constantly handled or used for paperweights) were a part of him, and he of them. The furnishings, from desks and chairs to ashtrays and wastebaskets, did not reflect the taste of a professional decorator, but had come to be there through an organic accumulation which centered around the personality of the inhabitant. The musical instrument was one that he played not to make people stop laughing, but for contemplation, excitement and solace.

Perhaps above all this was a world of contemplation. Not only the contemplation that looks out windows and dreams, but especially the kind that becomes involved in the sensitized manipulation of objects and instruments, the savor of discreet sensations, the critique of word and thought—in short, the play of the intellect as a sensuous experience. All this is very French, very urban, very Parisian, though it was the product of a thousand years of European cultivation.

Perhaps this will help to indicate how important the subject matter of Cubism really is. Just in itself it is far more significant than the subject matter of *Les Desmoiselles d'Avignon*. But it has another kind of importance in contrast with the earlier picture. In *Ma Jolie* the themes of Cubism become completely integrated with the style. What this means is that the same order of thematic values in the picture also determines the structure of the painting. This structure is a compilation in which a certain decision made at a certain point determines a later decision, and that determines another—much the same as in modern French life, with its tendency to be highly intellectual and procedure-conscious. Retaining a mellow, reflective quality, these pictures seem almost Old World today. They evoke the flavor of that most purely civilized tradition in Western history: Parisian society from Watteau to Talleyrand to Debussy.

One cannot overlook the quality of sensation in these pictures. Though there is a very strong element of drawing (which hardly existed in Impressionism), and although there are many fine Cubist drawings, this is still an art of painting. The quality of the substance, carefully yet sensuously modulated, not only corresponds to the mood of the subject, but even corresponds to certain aspects of Impressionist style.

Both styles tend toward a certain size of painting; the typical size might be approximately twenty by thirty inches. It is rare for either an early Impressionist or an analytic-Cubist picture to be very much larger or smaller. With the Impressionists, one might be tempted to ascribe this relatively modest size to the speed of painting; it takes time to cover a surface with paint, and after a few hours light conditions change. But in point of fact, even the Impressionists could not execute a painting in one sitting; presumably the artist returned to the subject under comparable conditions. And if an Impressionist picture was the product of a few sittings, a Cubist picture might take dozens; some are known to have taken a hundred. The explanation of this choice of size must be sought elsewhere. It will be remembered that with an Impressionist painting, the optimum viewing distance is roughly arm's length. Over that, one begins to miss the vibrant elaboration of the brush strokes; under that, the field of focus may be lost. Much the same is true for a Cubist painting. The arm's length is also the distance at which both kinds of painting were actually done (as is not true of many other kinds of painting). With both the Impressionists and the Cubists, the painting is of a size to be seen, touched, and by implication, held in the hands. It becomes an object to be held, cherished, even "touched" by the eye, much as the painter touched it with his brush. All this is very much a French way of thinking. The cherished object is held close, intimately; it is caressed with hand and eye; but always it is kept at a slight, discreet distance.

Intimate yet discreet—equally French were those otherwise-opposed styles Impressionism and Cubism. What has been said applies specifically to analytic Cubism, whose stylistic fulfillment may be dated from 1908 or 1909 to 1913 or 1914. Analytic Cubism represents probably the shortest span on record for a major style.

Cubism in the broad sense continues well into the 1920's, its later and longer period often being called "synthetic" Cubism. The distinction in terms is partially misleading. "Analytic" Cubism is in fact a highly synthetic style: all its aesthetic components are integrally related, the whole to the smallest part; these formal qualities, in turn, are perfect counterparts of the subject values expressed. But in terms of fragmenting the object, as well as breaking up the picture surface, the early form of Cubism appears much more analytical than the later.

In a "synthetic" picture by Picasso (Plate 10), the style is no more synthesized within itself or in relation to its subject matter than in the "analytic" *Ma Jolie*; instead, the forms are larger, simpler, more synthetic in appearance. The high tension between complexity and clarity in the early pictures could only be maintained so long. The later Picasso shows a relaxation of style, an easing of emotional pitch, in some ways a reconstitution of the object—though the object will never again be the same. In their mathematical proclivities, their shallow, interwoven and ambiguous space, as well as their subject matter, these are still Cubist pictures, but color has now returned, and a sunny air invades the somber, indrawn rooms of the earlier paintings. These too are fine pictures, and not so easy to grasp as they may look.

If one tries to reproduce such a painting, something of the subtlety and decision in relating part to part, part to border and part to whole can be appreciated. The parts are more specific now; for this reason the later style is the more accessible one, and therefore it is the later style which most directly influenced the decorative and commercial arts, an influence active for at least a generation.

On examining the Picasso synthetic picture more closely, one sees that against the essential warmth of the tablecloth, the artist has arrayed a range of colors and tones, from the brown of the table and mandolin to the pink of the fruit and wallpaper. With their arrangement in partially geometric shapes, these colors contribute a decorative pattern that sustains interest over the entire surface of the painting.

But the colors also symbolize certain values of human experience— values of the intellect and of the senses, playing upon one another rather as the objects and tones in the painting play against one another. As with analytic Cubism, a life of contemplation and manipulation is evoked. But here there is far more of the senses—of tasting and savoring, and specifically of reading, for the music sheet which dominates the center of the painting is echoed in the markings of the tablecloth and of the wallpaper.

Again, this is a world of wit and of unexpected reversals of normal experience, but the wit and the reversals are less abstract, more dependent upon the objects. Thus, the bust, which has a classical form, is black instead of the white of antique marble or modern plaster. Similarly, the lines of brow and nose are reversed. Color is once again bright, and not only articulates the parts of the composition, but evokes specific objective qualities. For example, the little spots of fresh color around the edge of the mandolin and up the frets convey a jingling sensation, expressing the quality of sound made by the instrument. And in the melon, the bands of thin, light, delicate tones give a blandness to the color which corresponds to the bland taste of a melon.

After the high tension and achievement of analytical Cubism, its difficult wit and sustained seriousness, there was a return to the imme-diacies of life, to joy and ease. It is worth noting that this turn came, not at the end of that war that devastated the old civilization of which the early Cubism had been a last echo, but at its beginning. Art, as it often is, was ahead of society.

VI WHAT IS ABSTRACT?

All genuine art is abstract. —SUSANNE LANGER

There is no abstract art. —PABLO PICASSO

This art which has been called abstract . . .
This art is concrete. —LE CORBUSIER

In the title of the preceding chapter it was intimated that Cubism is not abstract art. How can this be? Surely the entire history of Cubism from late Cézanne to *Ma Jolie* shows a progressive abstracting of the forms of nature.

The difficulty, alas, lies in the variety of meanings of the word abstract. To "abstract" originally meant to draw out or to remove. As applied to art, this would mean to remove or distill some significance from undifferentiated nature. As a noun, an "abstract" is a selection or summary, as in an attorney's abstract. In either of these related contexts one can certainly say that all art is abstract, since even the most proliferated forms in Gothic architecture, Indian sculpture or Baroque ornament are highly abstracted essences of some vital principle felt in nature.

As applied to art, however, there is a quite different meaning for abstract. This meaning is usually found in the adjective, for which a dictionary definition is: "separated from matter, practice, or particular examples, not concrete; ideal, not practical; abstruse . . ." It is this sense which is intended when we speak of much of the art of the twentieth century. Abstract art in our day does not mean "separated from matter," of course; nor does it mean "not concrete." What it means is "separated from" the recognizable object.

For this reason the term "non-objective" rather than "abstract" has often been used. It is more descriptive, though it suffers from being negative. It is not often used by artists, who generally prefer to call themselves abstract—possibly because the very term is abstract enough to foil further pigeonholing.

Thus, there is no real difficulty in the apparently conflicting statements of the aesthetician Susanne Langer and the artist Pablo Picasso. What Miss Langer means is that all art, even the most naturalistic, deals in "abstracting" meaning and form out of the chaos of worldly experience. What Picasso means is that no art, no matter how non-objective, fails to spring from vital experience or to embody crucial human issues.

The most "realistic" art of the Renaissance—when it is real art— makes compelling rhythms and arbitrary distortions, thus reaching a coherence, a readability and a *life as art*. The most non-objective art of our time—when it is real art and not design—is charged with feelings and responses, sensations and transvaluations, thus attaining a realization of *art as life*.

For these reasons there are some painters today who refuse to consider themselves "abstract." They would prefer to reserve the word for an artist like Josef Albers, in whose work the chief value lies in a manipulation of visual effects and experiments in design. On the other hand, such painters would not call the paintings of Mark Rothko abstract, because though his work is superficially similar to that of Albers, it vibrates with the mysteries of nature and of the human soul.

Such a meaningful distinction is in line with Picasso's view, reminding us that all true art is creative and can never stop at being illustration or design. But for our purposes it is a needless distinction. Still, the question of whether to paint from the object, no matter how apparently unrecognizable the result, or to paint "abstract" is a real issue.

As Jack Tworkov has said, it is essential that the abstract painting start by being abstract. This means that it cannot start with the object. Why? Because to start with the object or figure, to begin a painting by conveying something that comes specifically from life, is to give it an intolerable handicap: it predetermines the composition.

It is basic to this style of painting that the composition not be predetermined—that it be achieved as a part of the process of painting. Some artists feel that the painting actually takes over, takes on a life of its own, directs its own campaign. In comparison with most other styles, which start with a specific preconception, this is hardly an exaggeration. It represents only one side of the coin, however; the reverse is that what the artist has already done creates a state of tension or interaction with what he is in the process of doing. The dialogue of art, which in a Renaissance painting took place between actors on a stage, now takes place between the painter and the painting.

In true abstract art, the object or figure is not a source but a product of the painting. By this I mean that the picture begins with areas of color, motions of brush strokes, notations of rhythm and formal structure. Only as it develops do the artistically telling *configurations* emerge. These configurations show a certain character which, even more than in the Renaissance, identifies the artist beyond any need of a signature. With a Tworkov, a Pollock, a Robert Motherwell, the painting itself could be said to be the signing. Such artists are very much "expressionists," even though they usually emphasize the "abstract" when talking about art.

Here again is a close parallel between modern art and instrumental music. Even with the partial interruption of a programmatic tendency in nineteenth-century music, instrumental music in the West has been at the same time the most abstract and the most directly emotive of all arts. "Abstract Expressionism" is not only a rather good term for the best contemporary painting; it is also descriptive of modern art in general and of the direction in which that art has sought to find itself. Like instrumental music, abstract art is one of the art forms freest of the burden of conscious memory, and thus most open to a range and depth of suggestion.

This directly abstract art is very different from the type of "abstracting" that occurs so often in student work, and even in the work of some well-known artists. There is a great deal of this sort of painting to be seen or purchased all across the country, and its appeal probably comes from the fact that it satisfies two differing needs at once. One is that a picture contain references to a world of known objects; the other is that it look "modern"—meaning *à la mode*.

By starting with an object and then stylizing it so that a decorative pattern takes over, the painter provides the patron with something that is obviously "art," since it is stylized in some "modernistic" fashion, but at the same time comforts him with its suggestion of a horse, a tree, a woman or a coffee cup. Being so comforted, he may buy—but very likely he has not acquired a work of art. Art, and particularly genuine modern art, is not always comforting. Ours is an age which seeks its comfort in sex, alcohol, drugs or the analyst's couch, more than in cultural forms. We glory, or ought to, in the tension and complexity of the age, and as Trotsky once suggested, he who desires the life of ease does ill to be born in the twentieth century.

For anyone who really wants a work of art that is comforting in its specific reference to known objects, the best idea is to buy a half-decent Renaissance painting (these are not necessarily priced beyond average means). If it is any good as a painting, it will contain far more "ab-

Collection, Museum of Modern Art, New York

Solomon R. Guggenheim Museum Collection, New York

PLATE 17: Piet Mondrian, *Composition 7*, 1913. Oil on canvas, 41⅞″ x 45″

PLATE 16: Theo van Doesburg, top: *The Cow*, series of eight pencil drawings, n.d., 4⅝″ x 6¼″; center: *Composition (The Cow)*, 1916, gouache, 15⅝″ x 22¾″; bottom: *Composition (The Cow)*, 1916–17, oil on canvas, 14¾″ x 25″

stract" elements and relationships than may at first appear, but these abstract qualities will be integral to the representational elements, so that the picture will be meaningful as art. In contrast, an artificially stylized horse, in the "modernistic" manner, will probably come to look like what it probably is: a fraudulent amalgamation of photographic references and decorative patterns. Where there is no felt necessity in the relationship between form and theme, there may be artistry, but there can be no art.

Another questionable kind of abstraction can be systematically examined in Theo van Doesburg's "aesthetic transformation of the object" (Plate 16). Van Doesburg was a serious artist and aesthetician, related to Mondrian in the important movement of the 1920's called *De Stijl* ("The Style"); indeed, he was the chief energizer of that group and of the periodical of the same name. Unfortunately, seriousness, while essential, is hardly enough to guarantee art.

In the first abstraction of the cow, one can make out easily enough that it is a cow, as long as the drawing is beside it. Without the drawing, one might be as likely to envision some sort of steel structure. The light and dark shapes are still seen as light and shadow, and there are strong diagonals and occasionally even curves, both of which in themselves connote life and action.

The final abstraction (actually, these are only two of a series) almost entirely disconnects the various elements. Figure and ground have a new, floating relationship. All diagonals have vanished, and the strongest vertical and horizontal accents move away from a central object, out toward a border pattern. But still there remain reminiscences of the cow. The long top horizontal for the backbone, the broken verticals for the hind leg, the strong vertical for the foreleg, and the series of increasingly weighted shapes for the neck and head are discernible, and even a projecting piece in the lower right corner for the muzzle. The belly, which has developed from stage to stage not in its aspect of mass or volume but in its aspect of being suspended, is represented by a large light area.

Perhaps this is where the trouble lies: everything is "represented." These abstractions are more interesting in relation to each other than as individual statements. It is intriguing to see how the weights and accents have been abstracted from both the appearance and the idea of the cow. But is any one of these pictures really convincing in its own terms? Brueghel's *Seasons* or Monet's paintings of the Cathedral of Rouen are enhanced as a series; yet each painting can stand alone. Perhaps the real value in the Van Doesburg is literally to be found in the "aesthetic transformation of the object"—in which case we are presented with a process, not with a series of individual works of art.

Another difficulty is that the artist winds up with an abstract picture but does so only by "drawing" or distilling certain qualities from a specific object. Yet it has the *appearance* of being non-objective.

These are two very different kinds of abstraction, only distantly related. To distill from an object is very different from starting with no object at all. This distinction is not always clear to the layman, even to many an artist; yet it cannot be emphasized enough. In *his* strongly directed career Mondrian moved from the kind of abstraction which begins with an object to the kind which is truly non-objective.

Having begun with expressionist landscape, he turned to a formalization of trees. These are clearly abstractions of the first kind, and between them and the "plus-and-minus" pictures (Plate 17) is a considerable step. Sometimes he called these "wave" pictures, and although they were inspired originally by wavelike rhythms and patterns, the reference to nature is distant.

The paintings of Mondrian's mature style (Plate 18) are, without qualification, non-objective pictures, and they show none of that confusion between object form and painting form which injures the Van

PLATE 18: Piet Mondrian, Composition 2, 1922. Oil on canvas, 21⅞″ x 21⅛″

PLATE 19: Pieter de Hooch, *The Visit,* seventeenth century. Oil on canvas, 26¾″ x 23″

Doesburg; the latter suffers from the left-overs of its earlier stages. "But Mondrian, that great merciless artist," as De Kooning has said, "is the only one who had nothing left over."

Or one might say, "—nothing but life." For there is plenty of life in a Mondrian, even in his most purely non-objective, non-referential work (Plate 18). Here the process of abstraction is not worked out in a single exercise, but is the result of many years' wrestling with the problem of what an abstract painting is about. This might be called the internal aesthetic experience of the artist, and it is expressed in his settling on the pure use of primary colors, black and white, the square and rectangle, the vertical and horizontal, and the straight line alone.

But there is also an inner *emotional* experience in such a picture. For these elements are not merely logical; they are expressive. They are involved in the depth and expanse of a general experience of nature, but they may also be related through specific formulas. As Mondrian took it from the philosopher H.J. Schoenmaekers, the vertical equaled male-space-statics-harmony; the horizontal equaled female-time-dynamic-melody. It is not necessary to accept these associations in order to recognize that they were felt by the artist and became a part of the motivation of his art, an emotional experience internal to the painting.

There are also *external* emotional experiences in Mondrian's art. For all their Platonic purity of geometry, can these pictures be separated from the twentieth century—from the off-beat regimentation of modern life or the sparkling look of a city at night? Mondrian himself said, "It is . . . wrong to think that the non-figurative artist finds impressions and emotions received from the outside useless, and regards it even as necessary to fight against them . . ."

There is an external *aesthetic* experience too, in the incessant tension between two-dimensional and three-dimensional relationships, as well as the spatial tensions between the colors, which cannot be separated from the grid lines. These lines produce rhythmic intervals, or sometimes even a rotary motion, and there is still more tension between the finality of the elements and the fluctuation in their patterns. Finally, there are the surface dynamics, which keep all the elements in equilibrium. The work of an imitator is likely to look like a tired assortment of colored patches. Mondrian's hard-wrought compositions vibrate, each one new, in an ineluctable light.

A curious effect in Mondrian is the similarity of his mature style to that of medieval stained-glass windows. In each the pulsating rhythm of the structure, in terms of pure color, and a spatial vibration of radiant tones is held in taut balance by severe black frames. Similarly, with the later paintings of Seurat, the radiance in his foregrounds and the vibrations of color in his painted frames are reminiscent of still other examples of old stained glass. In such works both Seurat and Mondrian seem closer to the vital effect of that older art form than the more conscious attempts of Georges Rouault and certain other modern artists.

Finally, it is helpful to keep in mind that Mondrian was a Dutchman. There seem to have been two particularly striking and rather opposite types of Dutch artists. On the one hand is the temperament of Hercules Seghers, Rembrandt, Jongkind or Van Gogh. Here the artist is highly involved emotionally, and the art is full of fire and tension. The other Dutch temperament is cool, sober, detached, measured, and in appearance at least, economical. Prime examples would be Vermeer, Saenredam, Pieter de Hooch (Plate 19) and Mondrian. To examine the De Hooch arrangement of a domestic interior with its predisposition for stable, geometric forms is to have a natural introduction to Mondrian. Even the old Dutch tile, along with that love of light which is perennial in Dutch painting, the cleanness and precision that mark at least a major aspect of the Dutch mind and habit, the stubborn determination and persistence long a part of the national character—all these enter into the apprehension of a single modern abstract painting.

. . .

In distinguishing between the two kinds of abstract art, I meant to imply that only the non-objective is truly abstract in the way in which I shall continue to use the term. This is the reason for saying that Cubism is not wholly abstract. While there are some Cubist works (more often drawings) which seem to be investigations into pure form, the typical Cubist painting proceeds from the object.

An ultimate example of the second kind of abstraction, the true abstraction, can be seen in Malevich's *White on White* (Plate 8). This painting is like a disquisition on the question, What do we mean by a painting? It is as if the painter, having raised the question, were to answer that a painting is painted on canvas in oil with a brush. An important part of this picture is the feeling of the brushwork on the canvas—not brush *strokes* as personal calligraphy, but brush*work*, so the viewer can feel with his eye a texture that meets the quality of the pigment and the quality of the instrument halfway, with these in turn adjusted to the slight spring of the stretched canvas. But what is the color of canvas? White. Therefore, one must find in variations of white paint those qualities that harmonize with the color and texture of the white canvas.

But there is another dimension to the whiteness. As black is the absence of color, white implies the presence of all color, in the same way that sunlight, which we think of as white (compared with the blue or yellow of artificial light) actually contains all colors. But light is also lightness, and therefore "white on white" may have a number of ramifications: the white square on the white square, or light on white, or light on color, or white paint on white canvas.

The shape of the painting may be just as significant as the choice of medium or color. It is a square because that is the perfect rectangle and, at least in Western art, a painting is almost always a rectangle. Even the size (thirty-one and a quarter inches square) would seem to have been chosen for its manageability. So Malevich began with the perfect shape and size.

But, one might ask, What is the content of a painting? In 1927 Malevich wrote, "Every real form is a world. And any plastic surface is more alive than a [drawn or painted] face from which stare a pair of eyes and a smile." In this picture it is as if he were saying: if the surface is more alive than any simulation made upon it, then the surface itself may be the "subject" of a picture.

The subject is that to which the artist gives a color and shape—much as the poet gives it "a local habitation and a name." What is the shape of *this* subject (which is the surface)? Square. So the painting shall consist of a square inscribed within a square. Are these squares related? Yes, as the subject of a picture is related to the painting as an object. This relationship can be indicated by the touching—or near touching— of the squares.

Notice the element of choice here. If the painted square were set "squarely" within the painting, not only would "subject" and "object" not touch, but either the subject would pop out of the object or the object would dominate the subject. (This is a problem, I think, in the squares within squares of Josef Albers, and he solves it by the use of overwhelming color relationships which leave the elements of design relatively meaningless.)

If the subject square were placed with one side lying against the object square, the resulting imbalance would require color or some other factor for compensation. If the logic of relationships is satisfied by locating the subject square tangent (or nearly tangent) at one point on the object square, why then at that particular point?

For one thing, the result is interesting without upsetting the equilibrium. For another, the relationship of corners is rather complex. At upper left, the subject square is very nearly tangent to the object square —close enough to suggest that relationship without being so obvious or disturbing as an actual touch. At upper right, the distance still suggests the possibility of touching, but is so much greater that space flows around the corner. At lower right, the squares pull apart, and the surrounding space becomes activated. Finally, at lower left, the corner lifts up and seems to soar, a tendency which is contained, however, by the corner at upper left, which is tied to the object square, with its horizontal stability.

If this seems arbitrary, then try rotating the figure one side at a time and see how different are the experiences of space, motion, contingency, even weight. Seen upside down, the subject square seems to teeter insecurely on a corner; in addition, it suddenly looks like a box, and its upper edge seems to expand and become longer than the others. (The reasons for such visual responses are matters for psychologists; the artist is more concerned about *what* happens than why.)

Turned on either side, the subject square appears to throw the balance of the picture off to either left or right. With the right side up again, one experiences a very real sense of floating, a lightness, even a soaring, that maintains a fine tension with the heavy, squat qualities native to the square. Related precisely as they are, the subject square takes on a *contained* quality (meeting the requirement of giving form to the subject), and the object square takes on an *open* quality which permits the other to move in a kind of focused freedom.

It is now time to return to the brush stroke, which is the actual beginning of a painting. (The surface of a painting may be previously treated by priming or underpainting, but the decision-making does not begin until the brush is poised.) Although it also works the surface, still the brush, as the instrument of painting, like the pen in drawing, first of all makes a mark. And what is the purest form of mark? The line.

Pure line is a major element in the painting. But what is the most distinctive line? An edge. If the subject square were not a square, but a circle, some of this quality of line as edge would be lost. A circle has an edge in the sense that it has a border from which it can be cut out; but it does not have *edges*, each with its own direction, and each related in length to the other.

Perhaps the next most essential quality of a line is that it gives direction, and so in *White on White* the two qualities of line are embodied in their purest synthetic form. It should be noted, however, that technically the lines are not continuous or uniform. They are a series of small touches, the quality of "stroke," or brushwork, with which this discussion began. These touches permit the paint surface to fluc-tuate both among and across them. The result is an airiness suggestive of the molecular action of the atmosphere itself, or one might think of clouds—and this in turn evokes the symbolism of white as sunlight. So this most abstract, most logical exposition of what a painting might be turns out to have sensations and suggestions of nature. Like Mondrian, indeed like most modern artists, Malevich is a nature painter.

Malevich called this painting of 1918 a Suprematist composition. What he meant is best expressed in his own words: "For the suprema-tist . . . the proper means is the one that provides the fullest expression of pure feeling and ignores the habitually accepted object. The object itself is meaningless to him; and the ideas of the conscious mind are worthless. Feeling is the decisive factor . . . I perceived that the 'thing' and the 'idea' were taken to be equivalents of feeling, and understood the lie of the world of will and idea. Is the milk bottle the symbol of milk?"

Since Malevich objected to "ideas of the conscious mind," he might very well have objected to the sort of analysis of his painting that I have presented. There is always the danger of trying to read too much into a picture. Still, it remains the job of the critic to "read," to analyze and to articulate whatever he finds meaningful and relevant. In the end, *White on White* seems to me an exercise. Though it was done seriously and has value as a painting, it is not of the same order of significance or creativity as a De Kooning or a Mondrian.

The abstract art of Malevich or Mondrian is related in some ways to the still influential style called Constructivism. The idea that to produce art was to "construct" became a familiar concept among artists and critics during the first third or more of this century. Not only Mondrian, but some Cubists and other artists thought of their art as approaching the condition of architecture. While I think they were often mistaken, still Constructivist sculpture did have a kinship to architectural construction—and this may explain its failure or lack of interest as art. Modern architecture is a practical art, and modern painting and sculpture at their best are most impractical.

Like music. Schopenhauer called music the highest art because of its immediate grasp of pure essentials. The individual nature and accomplishment of abstract painting and sculpture may vary enormously, but it is in their kinship with music, and particularly with instrumental music, that one will find their dominant directions and their most vital meanings.

VII
EXPRESSING THE REAL AND THE SURREAL

Now, do you think I am mad, all of you? If I am, come and be bitten, for the vaccination of artistic madness is a good specific against the smallpox of wordly vanities. —SAMUEL PALMER

When you have to attend to . . . the mere incidents of the surface, the reality—the reality, I tell you—fades. —JOSEPH CONRAD

Generally speaking, abstract art concentrates on form; themes, in the ordinary sense, are muted or ignored. But abstract art is not the only important tendency in the twentieth century. At the same time that the Cubists and the non-objective artists were pursuing formal values (i.e., exploiting form), other "schools," especially the Expressionists, the Dadaists and the Surrealists, were exploiting more purely thematic motivations in their art.

The value of a theme in a painting is often called the "content"; the theme itself is merely the title or identification, while the content is a product of the theme and the special way in which it is developed. Clyfford Still has said, "When I look at Grünewald's *Crucifixion* [Plate 20], the sky grows darker, the Christ is never quite dead and the terrible anguish of the Magdalene with her soft white wringing hands—this for me is experiencing content in a painting." (This picture, like its prototype, the Isenheim Altar, is one of the superb expressionist paintings of all time.)

On the whole, expressionism comes from the North and East of Europe. Both French and Italian art have tended, over the centuries, to be more classical, more "formal." Expressionism is found in the Low Countries, in Scandinavia, in Spain (never really classical, and hence outside the Mediterranean tradition), and above all, in Germanic lands. The whole German school of the Renaissance was expressionist, and no artist more so than Grünewald; indeed, his expressionism was so pervasive, so natural and so inventive that compared to him, most of the modern Expressionists seem a little tame.

Expressionism is essentially a gothic trait, in the sense that Van Gogh is gothic. The word connotes wildness, energy and unease. It seeks the sublime rather than the beautiful; even the terrible rather than the lovely. Unlike the classical, it is an art of involvement and not detachment. From the restless style of the ornaments and artifacts of the earliest wandering Northern tribes down to the twentieth century, one can follow this wild will to art all over Northeastern Europe.

The Eastern is as important as the Northern. Twentieth-century Expressionism in Europe appears almost entirely east of the Rhine (an exception is the French painter Georges Rouault). In contrast to the clarity and idealism of the West (Italy, France and to some extent England), the East leans toward the mystical and the intensely real. These characteristics are part of the reason for the opposition of Expressionism to Cubism.

After Van Gogh, the most significant step toward modern Expressionism was taken by the Norwegian, Edvard Munch, who, though living and working long into the twentieth century, did some of his most important work in the late nineteenth. Reacting with Nordic fervor against the complacency and detachment, the domesticity, of French painting, Munch proclaimed in 1889, "No more interiors with men reading and women knitting shall be painted. They must be living people who live, breathe, suffer, and love. I will paint a series of such pictures; people shall understand the holy element in them and bare their heads before them, as though they were in church." This is what is meant by gothic spirituality—that strangely intense, deeply committed need to find the sublime, even in the most earthly themes. No longer medieval, this aspiration now seeks to realize its visible forms not in images of saints or the transcendent, but in the objects and people of this world. The aspiration to find the sublime in the mundane is a perfect description of Van Gogh's *The Potato Eaters,* which stands in the lineage of Rembrandt, in whom Van Gogh himself found "that tenderness in the gaze . . . that heartbroken tenderness, that glimpse of a superhuman infinite that seems so natural there."

Expressionist works are not so susceptible to the logical, systematic analysis that Cubism invites. In a lithograph like Munch's *Jealousy* (Plate 21), the rhythms of non-facial passages (falling hair, bodies and trees) take on an "expression" that corresponds to and intensifies the facial expressions. With these and with the brutally or delicately exaggerated drawing, the story is told. This picture is somewhat programmatic, and to that extent, limited as art. (Beethoven insisted that his own moods were general, not specific. Art cannot rest at the particular.) In the best works of Munch, the artist transcends a particular experience or mood and generates a universal response. In *The Shriek* (Plate 23) one can feel the psychic and historical desperation of modern man, alone in an expanding and shifting universe. Munch said, "I felt this great cry throughout Nature." Much that has been elaborated in existentialist literature and philosophy in our own time is expressed in this picture, and one is reminded of Picasso's statement that "I am always aware that I am engaged in an activity in which the brush can accomplish what the pen cannot."

In *The Shriek* the brutal lines in the area around the head and ears

PLATE 20: Mathis Grünewald, *The Small Crucifixion*, sixteenth century. Oil on panel, 24¼" x 18⅛"

seem to convey an almost unbearable anguish of sound. Elsewhere the sound waves swirl and echo unceasingly in rhythms that envelop and swallow man up without comfort or assurance. The unrelenting quality of the emotional tension is echoed in the precipitous rush of road and railing, at the end of which stand two anonymous figures, out of touch.

It was the woodcut, however, that emerged as the favorite graphic medium of Expressionism. Rejecting the almost limitless pictorial possibilities of lithography, which had dominated printmaking during the nineteenth century, the fluid and spontaneous felicities of etching and even the hard but complex refinement of metal engraving, the modern Expressionists revived the first and most forceful form of printmaking in the West: the relief-cut wood block. This medium satisfied their needs for blunt immediacy, simple directness, innocent anti-virtuosity and weightiness of treatment that corresponded to the weight of the themes.

A print such as Nolde's *Prophet* (Plate 22) exemplifies these qualities. Yet for all the genuine fervor of the work, it can never recapture the unthinking devotion and the unself-conscious expression of a sacred image that was spontaneous in the Grünewald (Plate 20). A twentieth-century work, if it is to be convincing art, cannot avoid the character of its own age; and thus, both the expression and the handling of form in any modern work betray a self-awareness which, however poignant and vital in its own way, is true to the time.

As the imagery in such works is manipulated and forced (often to powerful effect) rather than proceeding spontaneously out of heartfelt visions, likewise the handling of the medium, despite its avowed aim, always betrays a certain sophistication and virtuosity. The woodcut gave the Expressionists a perfect medium for mounting a slashing and aggressive attack on a large range of modern values.

In Nolde's *Prophet* the cut, slash and pare of the wood-block knife are complemented by strangely fluid areas which have the appearance of wash or stain. The result has almost as much the effect of a wash drawing as of a woodcut, so that while the medium is in one sense exploited, it is also overcome or transmuted. This never happened in the early woodcuts, which always bore the characteristic mark of their craft; though the medium was never exploited as an aesthetic element, neither was it suggestive of another medium. This is in no way a criticism of the Nolde—quite the contrary; it is entirely unified, and reminds us of what Rembrandt and Goya added, in their dark wash drawings, to the spiritually expressive graphic tradition of profound whites and blacks.

Not all Expressionist themes are concerned with the tragic or prophetic. Some, like Kirchner's *Five Women in the Streets*, Nolde's *Lemon Groves*, Otto Mueller's *Gypsies with Sunflowers*, suggest something of the richness of Expressionist imagery, and they range from urban sophistication and tension to primitive ease and exotic radiance. Almost all the artists were highly productive in portrait and landscape, and these two categories apparently found in Expressionism their last flowering in Western art. Of these, the portraits and landscapes of Kirchner—paintings and above all woodcuts—should endure as masterpieces of their genre.

The literary value in Expressionism is not confined solely to the painting. Sir Herbert Read, a literary as well as art critic, has written: "Nolde's autobiographical writings and his letters; Barlach's several dramas and his autobiography; Kandinsky's more theoretical works and his poems; Munch's poems; Hodler's writings and letters; all these, like the letters of Van Gogh, are works of art in their own right, and not mere documents."

If Expressionism revived a literary content in painting, and if it revived medieval techniques, still it was hardly a retrogressive style. Its sense of the anonymity and loneliness of man's identity is entirely modern, and its handling of paint and manipulation of color are not so far from the aesthetic of Matisse, though the tone is profoundly different.

In other respects it points toward contemporary things. Oskar Kokoschka's *Tempest* catches in swinging, embryonic rhythms the love of the artist and the widow of the composer Mahler. The dancing colors are ecstatic, yet sober and cool. The setting is a hyperreal dream world, and the figures seem billowed in the mountains of the moon. Both in the centrifugal action of the composition and in the supraworldly cosmic setting, such a picture approaches the condition of a Jackson Pollock (Color Plate 5), although its own ancestor might be found in such a work as Van Gogh's *Starry Night* (Plate 24).

Much as Van Gogh's art moves from absorption in specifically human themes in the early work to absorption in nature in the later work, of which *The Starry Night* is a good example, so Expressionism itself tends to travel from the object to the environment, from the mundane to the cosmic and from involvement in literal human situations to involvement in nature. Many of Kokoschka's later landscapes are so open and restructured that they have an almost abstract appearance. A similar kind of development is evident in some of Chaim Soutine's more sublime paintings, the "Ceret" landscapes; at such moments Expressionism, as anticipated by Van Gogh in *The Starry Night*, approaches a condition not so far removed from that very different kind of Expressionism known as Abstract.

If Expressionism brought the "real" back into painting, it did so emotionally. (Surely Goethe was speaking above all for Germans when he proclaimed, "Feeling is everything!") But the real also raised its head in another major tendency of the art of the first half of the twentieth century—in the movement called Surrealism. Not that either movement

PLATE 21: Edvard Munch, *Jealousy*, 1896. Lithograph, 18¾″ x 22⅝″

Collection, Museum of Modern Art, New York

PLATE 22: Emil Nolde, Prophet, 1912. Woodcut,
12⅝″ x 8¾″

summoned back the old "reality." Expressionism, for instance, is always arbitrary and loaded with exaggerations. In the best book yet on Van Gogh, Julius Meier-Graefe wrote, "It was Van Gogh's exaggeration that was so galling. He exaggerated here just as he had exaggerated as a missionary. He mistook ideas for facts, and assumed that the motives of other people were as simple as his own." This is a fair summation of the innocence and intensity of all worthy expressionism.

This tendency to transvalue is naturally joined to a yearning for old and far-off forms and an instinct for prophetic themes, whether in the choice of Biblical subjects or in a work such as Ludvig Meidner's *Burning City*, surprisingly catastrophic for 1913. Again one cannot overlook old Germanic preoccupations with destiny or with the apocalyptic.

Until the appearance of Surrealism as a school, the "real" had traditionally been located in the consciousness. Surrealism introduced an overtly new approach: one arrived at the real through interaction of the conscious and unconscious. The word "Surrealism" was coined by a writer, Apollinaire, in 1917, and the movement itself, the most literary of modern art forms, was established by another writer, André Breton, who issued the First Surrealist Manifesto in 1924.

Because the literary aspect of Surrealism, far more than that of Expressionism, takes a literal form, Surrealist pictures need little introduction. Whether dealing in specific, tangible objects, as with Salvador Dali, or with more abstract or dislocated ones, as with Miró, the scene and situation can ordinarily be identified. Since these relatively literal parts become related in realms of fantasy, their symbolism is more readily interpreted.

And since this age was acutely responsive to Freud, much of the symbolism is, in the most inclusive sense, sexual.

Sometimes, as in a painting by René Magritte or Giorgio de Chirico, an apparently hyperrealistic scene will contain one utterly incongruous element. The result is not merely shock for its own sake (a major twentieth-century characteristic), but the establishment of an entirely new scene, impossible to anticipate. De Chirico describes the nature of such an effect: "Sometimes the horizon is defined by a wall behind which rises the noise of a disappearing train. The whole nostalgia of the infinite is revealed to us behind the geometrical precision of the square. We experience the most unforgettable movements when certain aspects of the world, whose existence we completely ignore, suddenly confront us with the revelation of mysteries lying all the time within our reach and which we cannot see because we are too short-sighted . . ."

Since the Surrealists were so interested in abnormal or unexpected relationships, it is not surprising that they paid much attention to dreams and the dream world. Indeed, Breton wrote, in the form of a definition: "Surrealism rests on a belief in the superior reality of certain forms of association hitherto neglected, in the omnipotence of the dream, in the disinterested play of thought." To some extent, all Surrealist pictures are dream pictures, in that they stress incongruity, the inexplicable change of identity, obsessive symbols and the like. But a dream is very difficult to paint. For one thing, while the dream itself is visual, its elements are constantly transforming themselves, shifting in and out of time. A moving-picture apparatus might help, but the visual aspects of a dream would remain too amorphous, too simultaneous. Dali's intended dream worlds are not at all like dreams. Miró's pictures of the 1920's and thirties are closer to the qualities and sensations of dreams, but they are abstract in a different way; for all their suggestion of touching the unconscious, the forms have a superbly predetermined air.

In another section of his definition of Surrealism, Breton reveals a more significant use for the dream world and the unconscious in painting. Surrealism, he says, is "pure psychic automatism, by which it is intended to express, whether verbally or in writing, or in any other way,

PLATE 23: Edvard Munch, *The Shriek*, 1895. Lithograph, 13$^{15}\!/_{16}$″ x 9$^{15}\!/_{16}$″

the real process of thought. Thought's dictation, free from any control by the reason, independent of any aesthetic or moral preoccupation." It was in the introduction of automatic drawing (as described above by Breton) that Surrealism was to contribute the most to modern art.

Besides his more artificially conceived paintings, Dali did some very free and convincing etchings, chiefly in his early years. These works should be better known, and could help to salvage the reputation of the self-confessed exhibitionist. Starting with the work of André Masson, the process of the "automatic"—that is, drawing or painting directly out of the unconscious—descended to Jackson Pollock, who was able to filter the vast impetus of Surrealism into contemporary art.

Why surreal in art? Why real? What is the real? What did Kipling mean when he invoked "the God of things as they are"? Partly that in the practical world at the end of the nineteenth century, old values and attitudes—especially Romantic and ideal ones—were becoming severe impediments. As Victorian men of affairs discovered the harsh but refreshing realities of the new life, they called on art to express these values. But as André Malraux has observed, in the nineteenth century, for the first time, artists and men of power ceased to hold the same values in common. This gap has existed as a deep historical reality for almost two centuries, and there is little point in wasting time wishing it to close by itself. Art and society in our time are in two different camps. We may not be able to bring them closer together, but we can build a number of bridges between them.

One bridge can be constructed on the fact that both modern artists and men of affairs consider themselves realists. An abstract painter a realist? Certainly. It is in just this respect that a creative abstract artist distinguishes himself from a commercial designer. Mondrian said, "Abstract art is . . . opposed to a natural representation of things. But it *is not opposed to nature* as is generally thought." Or Picasso: "I try to

make my paintings as reliable as history and as picturesque as fiction."
Or Hans Hofmann: "The spirit of a work is synonymous with its
quality. The *Real* in art never dies, because its nature is predominantly
spiritual."

Clearly, artists are thinking of a different kind of reality than what is
ordinarily meaningful to businessmen or politicians or sociologists. One
essence of the artist's reality is contained in Géricault's remark about his
early-nineteenth-century contemporary Carle Vernet: "One of my
horses would have devoured six of his." Both artists painted horses
which looked very much like horses anatomically and texturally, but
Géricault meant that his horses were far more intense and vivid. To
draw a horse is one thing; to make it come alive is another. The difference is precisely that between craft and art, and it is that difference
which makes art indefinable. All we can say is that for something to
come out of a work of art, it must have gone into it. An old Indian
maxim says, that he who cannot *be* a tiger cannot draw one.

The Surrealists immediately perceived that realism in art is a tricky
matter. One can discuss the difference between representational art and
non-objective art; one can even define the first as dealing in "realism," as
opposed to the latter—though already this can lead to argument. But
one certainly cannot say that an example of representational painting is
more "real" than an example of abstract painting: whichever is more
real is always the one which is more real *as art*.

These distinctions are important in art criticism. But to return to the
subject of the *perception of reality* as dealt with by earlier representational art and by Surrealism, the latter school is saying that the most
"real" things one experiences are perceived in unexpected ways. Since
the unexpected in Surrealist works often takes the form of the impossible, one is confronted with an appreciation of truth which takes the
form of a lie.

This is not a new idea in art. Picasso has said, "Art is a lie which makes us realize the truth." And long before, in the early nineteenth century, the painter Jean Etienne Liotard said, "Painting is the most astounding sorceress. She can persuade us through the most evident falsehoods that she is pure truth."

This is not to imply that all reality in art is unreal. In fact, the vast art of the Renaissance—occasional tricks apart—was a reality that was just what it seemed, and was convincing as such because Renaissance realism was always in the service of a world in search of a tangible ideal. In the art of Donatello or Velasquez the real and the ideal are so reflective of one another as to be hardly distinguishable.

In modern art, however, realism could never attain such a concrete articulation, because neither the tangible reality in itself nor the ideal from which it would spring is natural to our way of thinking. Even the "Realism" of the mid-nineteenth century led inexorably into Impressionism. It is characteristic of modern experience that the realism of *things seen* must lead into the realism of *how* things are seen; the workings of an internal process replaced the description of an objective world.

Surrealism in the sense of *hyper*-realism is not brand new in the twentieth century. Its heritage goes back to the earliest days of modern art, with David, Goya, Füssli and Blake. It emerges again with James Ensor and Odilon Redon in the nineteenth century. This recurrent way of seeking the real says in effect that what man sees and touches will never suffice to describe his reality. The artist must go further—into the psychic meaning of things seen. Do we see things in the way they are related in nature or according to our own ways of relating them? Do we see with the conscious or the unconscious mind? What *is* the mind's eye?

In modern realism one is confronted with two kinds of exploration in vision: the one that elaborates with the inner eye and the other that explores the actual way we go about seeing. The Impressionists took a major step in this direction; Cézanne took another. Compare Raphael's *St. George and the Dragon* with a Cézanne still life. In the former the lance continues from one side of the body to the other, exactly as it should. It can be checked with a ruler, which is rather tempting because the accuracy makes the lance look a little peculiar. But when the edge of a tabletop disappears in a Cézanne, it reappears again at a different level, sometimes quite noticeably. This strange phenomenon is not disturbing, however, because looking at each part of the picture, one apprehends a different set of spatial relationships; within each set everything is adjusted to make visual sense out of complex juxtapositions; moreover, each set in turn is related to its neighbor. All this requires quite arbitrary manipulations of shapes, spaces, edges and levels so that they make sense not according to what we *know*, but according to what we *see*.

Does this mean that the Raphael doesn't make sense? Not at all. The Raphael is logically composed. One *knows* that the lance is correct, and this overcomes any possibility that for purely visual reasons it will look peculiar. Raphael was interested in working out a system of visual relationships based on what we know about what we see; Cézanne developed a set of relationships which tell us that we have not seen what we thought we had seen, and that we must now see as he wishes us to. Degas had much the same thing in mind when he said, "The artist does not draw what he sees, but what he must make others see."

Another important part of Surrealism—the element of play—betrays a strong reaction to the intense seriousness of Cubism. There is almost no vital human experience which does not find its statement in art. Thought and emotion, action and contemplation, commitment and detachment, the physical or the nervous, the soothing and the exciting, the impulse and the rule, all come to the fore in one style or another;

PLATE 24: Vincent van Gogh, *The Starry Night*, 1889. Oil on canvas, 29″ x 36¼″

and so, not surprisingly, does the element of play. The high seriousness of Greek-temple architecture and sculpture had its counterpart in the indecent humor of the wonderful vase paintings made in the shadows of those temples. And in Shakespeare and the most serious writers, the tragic and the comic cannot always be separated. It was with Dada, the short-lived but epoch-making movement that preceded and opened the way for Surrealism, that the element of play broke through the seriousness.

But the comic has many aspects. Playfulness—the bawdy scene, the ribald jest, the slapstick situation—is one form of humor. (Thomas Hardy went so far as to say, "There is no better sign of the vitality of art than the delight of its master spirits in grotesque.") Quite another aspect of the comic is seen in elegant wit, delicate banter or the incisive quip. In this sense Cubism too has humor, being saturated with wit. In the most austere analytic Cubist pictures of Braque or Picasso, the authority of form is constantly modulated by the wit of relationships. It is not the sort of humor that sets off uncontrollable laughter; in fact, there is nothing relaxing about it. It is Gallic, urbane wit which appeals to the mind; it depends upon highly intellectual and conscious discernments of unexpected formal relationships. Though it plays upon the complex subtleties of the relations between what we see and what we know, upon highly sophisticated ambiguities, it is not *play* in the usual sense of that term.

Play suggests a spontaneous, irreverent, diverting activity that is capricious and free. This was the main motivation of Dada, which disclaimed even art itself for being too conscious and too serious. Many of the qualities of play are to be found in the work of Paul Klee, who might therefore be classed with the Surrealists, and is often classed with the Expressionists, but does not really belong with either group.

Klee's works are many and mostly literary. His titles, written in German (he was Swiss), do not always come through in translation, because of a quality of association or wit inherent in the literary idiom. Yet one may feel he would have liked his works to stand by themselves. *Old Man Figuring* is a title barely necessary (Plate 25). That the man is old is evident; the "figuring" is indicated in the finger that touches the chin and in the articulation of the fingers rather as if they were counting. (Also the fingers have a kind of clawing or scratching quality, which is echoed pictorially in the horizontal scratches across the etched surface.) The nose projects inquisitively, and the ear is shaped like a question mark. The arcs of the collar lines and the skull have both a searching and a measured quality related to "figuring."

Across the picture, etched lines—running now finely open, now richly dense—pull the figure into a field of sensitive activity. These lines are evocative of the etching process (the scratching and inking of the medium), so that one identifies with the touch of the artist, but they also play a thematic role. Opening around the chin, nose or fingers—where the articulation of form is crucial—the lines become noticeably dense as they project from the mouth and directly below the nose, across the eyes and out from the brow, and behind the ear. The sense of hearing, smelling, seeing, even talking, is thus elicited, and all contribute to an air of brittle canniness often found in the aged. This is re-enforced by a wariness implied in the eyes and the ear, which seem to change the direction of their attention front and back. The old man, therefore, is not just figuring, for he conjures up a whole syndrome of activities and qualities. It seems idle to ask what such a work owes to Cubism, to Expressionism, to Surrealism. Instead, it seems more to the point to invoke Whitehead's dictum that only the whole is really real.

A climax in the reality discovered by the Cubists, the Expressionists, the Dadaists and Surrealists was arrived at in certain paintings of Picasso and Max Beckmann in the 1930's; I am thinking particularly of Picasso's *Guernica* (Plate 26) and Beckmann's *Departure* (Plate 27). They were conceived in a Europe tense and desperate as it moved toward full-scale resumption of the conflict that had been suspended in 1918.

In *Guernica* Picasso carried color to an extreme. His enormous painting is entirely in black and white, with relatively few mediating areas or shades of gray. What is the meaning of "black and white"? One implication may be sought in the everyday use of the phrase: "She sees everything in terms of black and white." Here simple alternatives are seen as violent extremes. And not only are they extremes, they clash—black versus white, night versus day, good against evil, life against death. The last contrast is not only allegorical, it is specifically connoted by the absence of color. What is the normal response to the word "color"? The yellow of sunshine, the blue of the sea, the green of growing things, the red of fruit and flesh—all of these manifest life. But what (in our culture at least) are the funereal colors? We say "white as a sheet," "deathly white," "black as death"; and we know the white of the winding sheet, the black of mourning.

"Black and white" has still another connotation when applied to the printed page, especially the newspaper: "It is all there in black and white." The implication here is of the record, the *truth*. The important areas around the left center of *Guernica* are painted like newsprint, and it is as if Picasso were saying, "The world *will* note what we say here, and it can never forget what they did here."

"They" were the fascist airplanes sent on a saturation bombing raid of a civilian target, the Basque town of Guernica, in 1937, toward the end of the Spanish Civil War. The brutality of the incident, combined with Picasso's strong Republican sympathies and detestation of violence, stimulated the artist to complete the picture in a few months. It was a prodigious effort, entailing hundreds of preparatory studies and stages.

It should be emphasized, however, that *Guernica* was not propaganda. In an interview after the war Picasso said, "No, the bull is not fascism, but it is brutality and darkness . . . the horse represents the

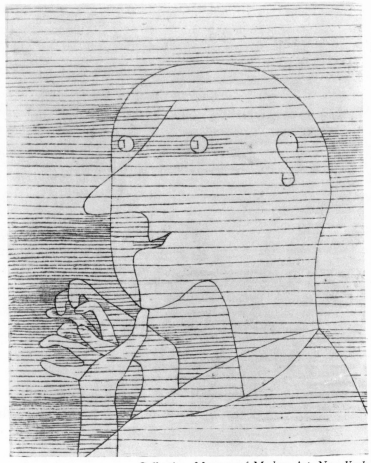

PLATE 25: Paul Klee: *Old Man Figuring*, 1929. Etching, 11¾″ x 9⅜″

people . . ." Elsewhere Picasso has emphasized that this painting is not so much a specific indictment as a general statement about war and atrocity, which is essentially the difference between protest and propaganda.

Stylistically *Guernica* may be considered a grand synthesis of cubist, expressionist and surrealist approaches. The narrow space, the sharp intersecting of planes and the severe schematizing of forms are all reminiscent of Cubism, as is the newsprint; but as used by Picasso, they are all singularly expressionist. In style, the "cut-out" quality of the bull is derived from synthetic Cubism, but its role is expressionist, and its meaning surrealist. Note how the many traditional associations of the bull—as symbol, emblem and actor, as hero and antagonist, as noble and destructive—are all intertwined. As a male symbol, the bull stands for exuberant life; yet he also stands above a screaming woman with a dead child in her arms. The setting itself is ambiguous. Though the bombing took place in the late afternoon, in the painting the scene is at night; at the same time a play of indoors and outdoors is elicited with an eerie unreality. The flames at right are shaped like teeth or tongues—appropriate enough when it is remembered that we speak of "tongues of flame" or of their capacity to "lick" at things. The actual tongue at center in the horse's mouth is rendered like a sharp instrument. S.J. Perelman once wrote of swinging out of bed at night to land on an apricot poodle which let out a needle-sharp yelp. Here is just such a metaphor: the piercing stab of the horse's scream is conveyed in the shape of the tongue and its relation to the swollen throat.

Between the horse and the bull is a light shape which from a distance looks like an airplane but can be identified close up as part of a bird. A spear pierces the horse ("the people") and leaves its striking marks upon the newsprint. Overhead a glaring light echoes the horse's scream. Its radiating beams are suggestive of the sun; yet the scene is nighttime, suggested by the lamp bulb at the center, which in turn resembles the pupil of a great, all-seeing eye, for the light is almond-shaped. The whole passage cannot be considered a specific analogy, but is rather a pictorial situation rich in ramifications.

At the right of the painting a woman drags her wounded knee, which sags, heavy as cement, to the ground. At lower left is a fallen warrior hacked to pieces. A dismembered hand holds a broken sword, but also, emerging almost surreptitiously, a single small flower springs from the hand into a beam of light. It seems rather like an anticipation of James Thurber's *The Last Flower.*

Beckmann's *Departure* (Plate 27) is also a synthesis of abstract, surrealist, and expressionist factors. It is a triptych—a form revived from the Middle Ages, in which three separate paintings are joined, with the center one dominating. Unlike medieval art, however, its symbolism is implicit rather than explicit. The fish, for example, which occurs again and again in *Departure,* is never the literal equivalent of Christ that it was in Early Christian art; Beckmann's use of it in symbolic situations (the ax head in the left panel, and the chieftain's helmet in the center, among others) indicates that the artist is referring to *symbolism as such.* Kandinsky once said, "Modern art can be born only when signs become symbols." This suggests that the modern "symbol" is unlike the older one, which served as a sign pointing to an original or as an emblem replacing it. The modern use of symbolism is broader, with ambiguity and suggestiveness in place of the old specific analogy and exact correlation.

The same kind of thing is found in works of Klee; for example, an arrow does not seem to stand for something or go anywhere; it is just there. Visually it is related to other signs in the painting; it is the "signness" that counts. And so in Kandinsky's sense it carries the value of a symbol.

The three panels of *Departure,* singly and together, must in the end speak for themselves; but it is possible to suggest certain specific interpretations.

PLATE 26: Pablo Picasso, Guernica (mural), 1937. Oil on canvas, 11'6" x 25'8"   On extended loan to the Museum of Modern Art, New York, from the artist

Clearly, the two side panels cast opposing reflections on the central and concluding panel. Themes of social and personal stress, chaos, torture, imprisonment and execution play against one another. The left panel seems particularly concerned with what man does to woman; the right, with what woman does to man. While they are broad in their implications, they are probably not political in the sense of referring to specific situations. It is sometimes said that the drummer in the right panel looks something like Goebbels, and such an interpretation is tempting, but considering the date of the picture (1932–33), it seems unlikely. A more probable association comes from Beckmann himself, who spoke of that corpse of our memories, wrongs and failures, from which we can never be free "while Life plays the drum." And speaking of the two side panels, Beckmann observed, "Life is what you see right and left. Life is torture, pain of every kind—physical and mental—men and women are subjected to it equally."

Emerging bright and bold, clear and hopeful, in contrast to the side panels, and relegating them toward the margins of life, is the central panel. At its own center is the woman Beckmann identified as the Queen (otherwise identified as the artist's wife). Although the mother-and-child theme is important in *Departure*, this is clearly not a Madonna. Beckmann felt that the Queen "carries the greatest treasure—Freedom—as her child in her lap. Freedom is the one thing that matters —it is the departure, the new start." Herein lies one meaning of the title.

And herein lies an allegory that would make the picture "subversive" in Hitler's Germany. But its meaning to the artist was more than political; it was in fact philosophical. In an implied contrast of the side panels with the center one, Beckmann said, "I assume that there are two worlds: the world of spiritual life and the world of political reality. Both are manifestations of life which may sometimes coincide but are very different in principle." The anguish of this irreconcilability—for all the occasional "coinciding"—might be considered a further theme of the painting.

The history of *Departure* is interesting. In 1937, distressed at the implications of the "Degenerate Art" exhibition in Munich, which displayed ten Beckmanns, the artist left for Holland, never to return to his native country. He took *Departure* with him, retitling it *Scenes from Shakespeare's Tempest* to deceive the Nazi censors. The painting subsequently came to America and is now in the Museum of Modern Art in New York. Beckmann came to the United States after the war and spent the last years of his life here.

Is it possible that there is an unconscious prophecy in this saga of artist and picture? In another comment about the title Beckmann said, "Departure, yes departure from the illusions of life toward the essential realities that lie hidden beyond." In the light of this remark, it is interesting to re-examine the closed form of the side panels and the opening out in the center one. Consider the grimness of the subject matter on either side: mutilation and execution on the left, blindness and despair on the right. In the center, however, a bright sky over a blue sea and the forthright movement of man and boat seem to signify a way out.

Is there a direction of movement here? Most people see the boat as moving from right to left; this would be consonant with the sweep of oars, arms and nets. Considering that *Departure* was painted in Europe, such a direction would be from east to west. Moreover, this was one of those moments in European history when the Old World called out to the New for aid and hope. Like the Norsemen of a thousand years before, Beckmann's monumental figures seem to strike out, ever westward, toward a land of promise.

One might add, as an historical footnote, that with such art, early in the 1940's the leadership of the Western world in painting passed to the American continent.

VIII

ABSTRACT EXPRESSIONISM

Reality . . . by all means more of it and not only in painting! The Common Man himself could use quite a bit—and above all the conservative critic. —HAROLD ROSENBERG

There is no subject matter to be discounted. It is all form and significant content. —GOETHE

Kandinsky's *Improvisation 28* (Plate 28) was completed in 1912. At that time it was considered audacious, for it seems to have little or no recognizable subject matter. Unlike the Cubism of the period, it is for the most part a non-objective painting. The subject matter is, in effect, purely the orchestration of lines, shapes and colors.

Compare with this another non-objective painting which also emphasizes pure line, color and movement, is also signally free in approach and inspired in handling, and like the Kandinsky, represents a major breakthrough. Jackson Pollock's *Lavender Mist* (Color Plate 5), measuring over seven feet tall by almost ten feet wide, was painted in 1950. Each painting explores pure color in both lines and patches, each develops a floating space with cosmic overtones, each produces forms which transform themselves as the painting develops, and each is graced with swinging rhythms that excite and tones that charm.

Yet there are vast differences between the two. In the Kandinsky the

Collection, Museum of Modern Art, New York

PLATE 27: Max Beckmann, *Departure* (triptych), 1932–35. Oil on canvas, center panel: 84¾″ x 45⅜″; side panels: 84¾″ x 39¼″

color is often located in a given area (though usually without any line around it) or else in congealed streaks or patches. For all the freedom of the painting, there thus remains a certain sense of conscious method; incidences and variations can almost be counted, if not predicted. Though not given to objects, the painting nevertheless retains certain objectlike characteristics.

In the Pollock, on the other hand, the color is an unexpected product of lines and stains. Though a sense of color can be traced throughout the picture, no single color has a definable location. Where the color in the Kandinsky is either contrasted with or specifically related to the lines, in the Pollock it is at once the same as and different from the lines: the two seem to come and go before our eyes. In *Lavender Mist* color has virtually rid itself of boundaries; it has no spatial definition or location.

Consider the use of line in the two paintings. In the Kandinsky, the line though free and unexpected frequently forms coherent shapes, intervals that are measurable, or traveling lines with a given pace. Moreover, these measurable qualities become objectlike in being countable: in one passage there may be four parallel strokes, in another, five radiating strokes; and in certain passages the three primary colors are juxtaposed in deliberate, studied quantities. In addition, some of the configurations carry unavoidable suggestions of objects out of life. I say "suggestions" because they are not really identifiable. But forms like "arms" may appear, or stockinglike shapes, along with splashes of sunlight or of celestial phenomena.

In contrast, the line in the Pollock seldom permits a configuration or measurement, much less a suggestion of objectlike character. Line in the Pollock consists of skeins of color thrown over a constantly changing surface. Yet the sense of line is overwhelming; indeed, it is the fundamental element of the painting. But it is a line which defines itself as perhaps never before: now a stroke, now a run, now a convolution, now a dash; here grouping in strong clusters or emphatic galaxies; there spurting out into open space, leaving behind nothing but a delicate comet's trail. Line upon line, line interfused with line, line overcoming line; line as color, line as black, line as white; line as motion, line as emotion; line that in all its complexity remains spontaneously clear and articulate, even strangely simple, as if to say that it is only a symbol of the myriad cosmic complexities, the unlocatable and immeasurable immensities that lie behind and beyond our tired world of objects.

But the world of external nature is not, for the modern mind and the modern artist, distinct from man, for the two interact and mirror one another. If at one moment Pollock seems to take us along clouds of stardust or into the pellucid depths of the sea, at another or even the same time we might be reminded of Sir Charles Sherrington's fascinating description of the human body as it awakens: ". . . the great head-end which has been mostly darkness . . . becomes now a sparkling field of rhythmic flashing points with trains of travelling sparks hurrying hither and thither. The brain is working, and with it the mind is returning. It is as if the Milky Way had entered upon some cosmic dance.

"Swiftly the head-mass becomes an enchanted loom where millions of shuttles weave a dissolving pattern, always a meaningful pattern though never an abiding one; a shifting harmony of sub-patterns. Now as the waking body rouses, sub-patterns of this great harmony of activity stretch down into the unlit tracks . . . Strings of flashing and travelling sparks engage the lengths of it . . . the body is up and rises to meet its waking day."

The comparative sizes of the Kandinsky and Pollock are related to the sense of space in the respective paintings. Though the space in the Kandinsky is open and unconfined—even unlocated in a cosmic sense—

the scale remains strangely intimate. The size of the Pollock is far beyond that of the human figure or even its reach. It therefore attains a scale beyond human measurement and puts man in a new spatial realm, just as there are no forms in the painting which permit recollection of familiar objects or empathy with human norms. Instead, the viewer must empathize with no less than universal space, with endless unravelings and ever new groupings in changing contexts.

It is important to observe that this particular quality of immensity is not attributable solely to the size of the painting. There have been larger oil paintings on canvas in the past, notably those of Veronese and Tintoretto in the Renaissance, but also by nineteenth-century Americans such as Frederick Edwin Church or Albert Bierstadt. The latter created spatial immensities that are not unrelated to that Western American expansiveness which was revived in Pollock. But in all these earlier pictures the pictorial space was fundamentally different from his.

With either a Tintoretto or a Bierstadt, one must stand at a significant distance from the painting in order best to apprehend the composition and realize the scene. With *Lavender Mist*, however, we are *drawn into the painting*. From a distance the pattern fascinates, but it cannot really be made out, and we are pulled closer and closer until the swirls of line and skeins of color emerge as specific elements; and still we cannot stop until the specific quality of the paint—dripped, poured, brushed, flung or traced—presents itself face to face. Or hand to hand, for at this point there is a growing empathy with the very manipulation of the paint.

But when the painting is approached this closely, something else happens. Being so near, we can no longer establish its boundaries; the space now passes beyond us—and far beyond the previous concept of a confined scene. And as it goes beyond on the left and right, and above and below, it also reaches out behind and envelops us. There is no longer a "picture plane" in the older sense of the term, no longer a simulated

PLATE 28: Wasily Kandinsky, No. 160b (Improvisation 28), 1912. Oil on canvas, 44″ x 63¾″

plane of action across the painting to which the spectator can simultaneously relate himself and the space within the picture.

Examined very literally, the space of this picture is rather shallow. There are certain veils of color and substance, certain veins of line and activity; there is no specific depiction of a deep penetration of space. Yet so expansive are these artistic elements in their vibrancy and inner relationships that we feel in the presence of the outer space of an expanding universe, one that takes us up in it, absorbs and transforms the human element—just as the aesthetic elements themselves have here transformed the art of painting.

The Kandinsky, by comparison, seems almost quaint—a refined, contained object of the Old World—though in its own time it was shockingly revolutionary and abstract. It is not just a matter of the degree of abstractness, or non-objectivity, that counts in two such paintings, but the *kind* of abstraction, its context and function. As Kandinsky shocked with his "musical" transformations of painting, so Pollock shocked with the violence of his attack on the very art of painting. As he himself described it, "My painting does not come from the easel. I hardly ever stretch my canvas before painting. I prefer to tack the unstretched canvas on the hard wall or the floor. I need the resistance of a hard surface. On the floor I am more at ease. I feel nearer, more a part of the painting, since this way I can walk around it, work from the four sides, and literally be *in* the painting." The importance of this in relation to the spatial experience of the resulting painting is obvious. (It is not an entirely new technique, Pollock pointed out; this was also the method of the Indian sand painters of the West.)

"I continue to get further away from the usual painter's tools such as easel, palette, brushes, etc. I prefer sticks, trowels, knives, and dripping fluid paint or a heavy impasto with sand, broken glass, and other foreign matter added." In point of fact, Pollock did not always use these new instruments and techniques. In many of the most beautiful pictures of his last years he returned to painting in oil with brushes. But a new realm of technique, as well as a new realm of space, made him a pioneer.

Jackson Pollock, Willem de Kooning, Franz Kline and others are best known as Abstract Expressionists, although sometimes they have been called "action" painters. The term "action" applies well to much of the work of Pollock, but it is not very descriptive of most of the work of the other leading practitioners of this school. Pollock worked at great speed and with an intense commitment to the action itself. In his method there was little room for preconsidered judgment or studious repainting. But this does not mean that his art is nothing but a wild gesture. On the contrary, the Pollocks we see are the ones that worked. There were others which did not. This waste is in the nature of artistic productivity. As Pollock himself described it, "When I'm *in* my painting, I'm not aware of what I'm doing. It is only after a sort of 'get-acquainted' period that I see what I have been about. I have no fears about making changes, destroying the image, etc., because the painting has a life of its own. I try to let it come through. It is only when I lose contact with the painting that the result is a mess. Otherwise there is pure harmony, an easy give and take, and the painting comes out well."

The public, at first appalled by the "violence" of Pollock's paintings, has widely come to see the actual dominance of that "pure harmony," that "easy give and take." The late dean of Italian critics, Lionello Venturi, thought Pollock, of all contemporary Americans, to be "the most passionate; his work goes beyond all passion to create gentle, tender arabesques and colors. And going beyond is beauty." (Compare the Louis Sullivan, Plate 29.)

But the lyrical grace of much of Pollock's best work should not blind us to its inescapable violence. The violence is there, but it is there rather in the approach to painting, even to art history, than in the individual canvas. As Willem de Kooning (who ought to know) said, "Jackson

PLATE 29: Louis Sullivan, architectural detail, *circa* 1900. Bronze

broke the ice." And indeed, Pollock's plunge into new possibilities of space and scope, of approach and technique, was so violent that for all the reactionary movements since, the old order has never been restored. In subsequent painting, object and space have new identities in themselves as well as new interrelationships, and there is usually little room for that caressing of the stretched canvas with which European masters from Giorgione to Matisse had made ineffable music. The violence and the destructiveness are found in the life of the artist as well as in his art. The parallel to Van Gogh is striking. With Van Gogh the emotional trauma, and with Pollock the nervous strain, of the effort to remake art and to oblige man to confront a new reality was cataclysmic. Each paid with his life.

But what a tender beauty resides in the work of each. Has anyone painted with a purer, less calculating love than Van Gogh in his orchards? Or with a gentler, more touching grace than Pollock in some of his "landscapes"? Whoever has lost himself in a maze of small branches

Schlessinger and Mayer Department Store

through which birds make their way in discriminating yet unpredictable rhythms will feel at home in *Lavender Mist*. The title, like most of Pollock's, must have followed the painting; clearly he began with no objectified orchard in early morning bloom. Yet when Helen Frankenthaler, visiting some years ago in Provincetown, awoke one morning to see through large glass windows the incredibly rich, delicate glow of the intertwined vines and rough foliage of this mid-ocean dune, bathed in a radiant dawn, her comment to her hosts was, "I didn't know you owned *Lavender Mist!*"

With Mondrian and Kandinsky it became clear that abstract painting in our world is anything but superficial decoration or mechanical exercise—that it is always nature painting. It should be equally clear that this does not mean that modern painting is necessarily *from* nature, but that it is *of* and *in* nature. This is part of the significance of Pollock's participation "in" his paintings; it corresponds to his realization of himself in and through nature. But this definition of nature by no means limits the artist to "nature study"—as in flora and fauna, rocks or water. Rather, it ranges through the entire cosmos of forms intuited or envisioned by the artist, from the microscopic to the macroscopic, with ever developing apprehensions of the nature of time as well as of space, and with ever new images of the place of man in a bewildering universe.

Because the nature content is so persistent in abstract art, one can better apprehend the painting of our time by examining nature in new ways: by looking up into the tracery of branches or down into the inner structure of a leaf; by absorbing the color and light vibrations when you're swimming under water, or the shapes of rocks and weather-beaten wood along a shore, or the land as seen from the air. From twenty thousand feet the interval and patterns of breaking waves are reminiscent of the "wave" paintings and others of Mondrian. I do not know whether Mondrian saw the sea from any such height, but it probably wasn't necessary; I have seen paintings by artists who had never been off the ground which look like nothing so much as aerial views of land or snow. It is the intuition that counts. And artistic intuition can operate both in relation to physical nature and to the history of art. Leonardo da Vinci made a topographical drawing which not only anticipates the topographical map but also has an astonishing resemblance to several characteristic practices of recent painting.

Another possible approach is to consult a good book of modern nature photography, not only for new worlds of visual experience in nature, new worlds of scale or morphology, but also for an automatic introduction to modern painting. None of this will say much about painting as an art— as creating something—but it can tell a great deal about the ways in which, consciously and unconsciously, modern art appeals to nature.

Nature remains, however, a field of exploration. A scientist may say (and more than one has), "Nature is quite enough for me." But when the artist explores, the true subject is the explorer himself, his psychic condition, his emotional experience, his ultimate transvaluations. For art never wholly departs from man. And just as the modern artist "explores" outer space, he penetrates the depths of his unique inner life. Robert Motherwell has said, "If a painting does not make a human contact, it is nothing . . . Through pictures our passions touch. Pictures are vehicles of passion, of all kinds and orders, not pretty luxuries like sports cars . . . The act of painting is a deep human necessity, not the production of a hand-made commodity."

By way of example, Motherwell recounts, "I respect a collector who returned one of my 'abstract' pictures to the gallery, saying it was too tragic in feeling for her to look at it every day. But somewhere there is a man with a tragic sense of life who loves that same picture, and I think he will find one day a way to have it. These are real human contacts, and I love painting in that it can be a vehicle for human intercourse . . . True painting is a lot more than 'picture making.' A man is neither a decoration nor an anecdote."

For a contemporary artist to speak thus should not be taken as a sort of compensation for the "abstractness" of modern art. In the best abstract painting the human content is hardly less important than it was in the humanistic art of the Renaissance. The external images are missing, but the assertion of values and the communication of poignant issues and true feelings, having been abstracted and purified of any association with objects, is still more direct. Even the most profoundly spiritual and intimate works of Michelangelo, Titian and Rembrandt carry allegorical freight that makes the communication of their emotions belong to a different order. This is not to say modern painters are greater; the artists mentioned above are almost without question the supreme masters of painting and sculpture in the entire Western tradition. The comparison is made only to convey something of the unparalleled directness and uncompromising purity of the way the modern artist probes his own soul.

There has been a good deal of comment about those aspects of contemporary painting which reflect an age highly attuned to depth psychology and to the exploration of the unconscious. But these facets of modern art are too vast for consideration here. To date, most psychological studies of artists have been undertaken either with inadequate command of psychological or medical knowledge on the one hand, or of art history and environment or artistic process on the other. The development of psychoanalytic techniques, combined with a solid background in the sociological history of art, would seem to be one of the most promising areas for future art criticism. This applies both to further understanding of the Leonardos and Van Goghs and to an exploration of those twentieth-century artists in whom the line between conscious and unconscious activity seems increasingly to be erased.

Meanwhile, the primary purpose of critic and layman alike remains not so much to analyze a picture as to discover its values through living with it.

The people who knowingly buy or return a Motherwell have not analyzed it; they have lived with it. This is very much a give-and-take proposition, and the reward to the spectator is in direct proportion to his effort. But no effort of this kind is effective without sympathy and a willingness to respond. To keep asking, Is this all a put-up job? is to guarantee getting very little out of modern art.

The memorable contemporary artists are utterly, sometimes painfully, sincere, at least about their art. And so their art should be approached with comparable freedom, courage and directness. No recent artist was more striking in these qualities than Franz Kline. Working for most of his career in black and white, Kline achieved a painting style monumental and intimate, simple and complex. Much less of the original is conveyed by a small black and white reproduction (Plate 7) than one suspects until he actually sees the painting. For these are real paintings, in the sense of the distinction made earlier between drawing and painting. First of all, the sheer size of the canvas counts. It counts spatially, as it tends to envelop man's small stature and expand his reach. And it counts in the felt weight of massive blacks resounding with imperial whites. (Where Malevich painted white on white, Kline painted white on black on white).

Without beguilement of color, the text of Kline's grand sermons presents issues of thick and thin, of heavy and light, of matte (that is, dullness) and gloss, of rough and smooth, of areas that are loaded or floating. All these polar possibilities—and many others—in the sheer handling of paint in its most direct form are pursued and forged into a new order of experience.

But this is not manipulation for its own sake. The beauty and clarity might be only a game were it not for the nobility of Kline's pictorial gestures. The expansive attitudes, the dramatic stature, of these forms, are like the very sweep of the artist's own stature and gesture in life— bold and free, strong and gentle, unexpected and sure.

From means apparently—even insistently—simple, Kline developed an armory of elements strikingly rich and complex. To be confronted with the original painting is to become aware of the changing velocity of the brush stroke, the disciplined but comprehensive gradations in tone, the sliding of masses one into another, the twisting energies that emanate from slashing whites and merging blacks, the jagged juxtapositions played in melodic counterpoint with fuzzy fadeaways—all resulting in a giant harmony of disparate elements.

On occasion critics have found Kline's paintings violent, even brutal. It is true that to be surrounded by a roomful of Klines is to know the hurricane in the heart; yet in every powerful confrontation there is grace; in every slashing conflict, the ease that comes of resolution. It is the ease of command, of the born painter, of the man of such magnitude that private distress could not intrude into the development of the work he loved. The magnitude and the gesture in his art are profoundly stamped with the inner quality of the man. Surely it was for such a reason that Munch referred to Van Gogh as a "great man" rather than a great artist, though the latter was obviously included.

But these are not the only sources of meaning or value in Kline's art, for he too is a nature painter. Reacting as a twentieth-century city dweller against the nineteenth-century nature cult of Thoreau, Kline found nature not in trees and ponds but in railroads, bridges, trestles and piers, and above all, in the organically changing "landscape" of New York as a city. "When I look out the window—I've always lived in the city—I don't see trees in bloom or mountain laurel. What I do see—or rather, not what I see but the feelings aroused in me by that looking—is what I paint."

Though less revolutionary than Pollock, less complex than De Kooning, Kline combined strength and sureness, simplicity and authority, ease and purity, all in a continuously evolving and directed style that in these respects has no counterpart in recent painting. It could be argued that Kline is the most American of painters since Albert Ryder and Thomas Eakins, at the turn of the century. His insistence on the black and white is important in this connection, for the black-and-white instinct is very old in American art. Indeed, it could be claimed that Americans have not primarily been colorists.

Nevertheless, in his later years Kline was working in an increasingly effective color vocabulary. His last painting (Color Plate 11) is an apotheosis. Other contemporary Americans are fine colorists: Jack Tworkov (Color Plate 8), for example. His paintings since the 1950's are as strong and vibrant as any, American or European, combining a strong diagonal virility with a rich radiance of solar color and light. In the recent work of Fritz Bultman (Color Plate 7), immense luminescences of sea and sky are interpenetrated with depths of color that seem to come from *behind* the atmosphere, or far within the rich depths of the sea. Seemingly in the tradition of the later Monet, Bultman's development of color fuses recollections of external nature with impulses and deep sensations of inner experience.

For the use of color in its own terms—as a subject in itself—Giorgio Cavallon is a contemporary master (Color Plate 6). In his paintings color is employed in almost every way possible in abstract art, playing role after role simultaneously, especially in terms of location and juxtaposition. With Cavallon the color white—for here it is truly a color—does not merely take on substance and light; it becomes a summation or embodiment of *all* color: this is not a treatise on white, as in the Malevich, but white seen as a unique property, explored as an object of love.

With these artists, or with Rothko, De Kooning, Bradley Walker Tomlin and Clyfford Still, America has made major contributions to the use of color, that element in the art of painting which is likely to be—Matisse said it *ought* to be—the last to reach full development. Color as a decorative factor is accessible to any sensitive eye, but color as light, color as space, color as an active agent in the composition—these are difficult and sophisticated experiences. "A factual identification of colors within a given painting," warns Josef Albers, "has nothing to do with a sensitive seeing nor with an understanding of the color action within the painting."

Color as light was a principle of early Impressionism. Color as space was encouraged by Cézanne and has become an integral function of modern painting, connecting such otherwise different artists as Matisse and Mondrian, or Rothko and De Kooning. What perspective was to the expression of space in the Renaissance, color has often been to the energetic spatial vibrations of modern painting. Yet for the Westerner the experience of space has always been actively emotional, and so contemporary color joins two factors: objective spatial suggestion and subjective emotional articulation.

Space in Abstract Expressionist painting is usually inseparable from the experience of the painting's surface. Spatial pattern and surface pattern, spatial activity and surface activity, even spatial existence and surface existence—which is to say, both the visionary and the tangible elements of the painting—interact and depend upon one another. The surface of a painting, said Hans Hofmann, is a "world in itself—or you may call it, more modestly, only an object, or simply a picture with a life of its own—a spiritual life—through which it can become a work of art." So the painting's tangible surface can, like the space within the picture, take on a visionary or "spiritual" dimension through its capacity to transform dead material into life.

It is above all in the activity of the surface that one becomes aware of modern painting as an object of process. While this aspect of painting reaches its apogee in Abstract Expressionism, it is implicit in many other styles of the past century. Even an artist so classical by nature as Georges Braque has stated: "In painting there must be no preconceived idea. I could not do otherwise than I do. The picture makes itself under the brush. I insist on this point. There must be no preconceived idea. A picture is an adventure each time. When I tackle the white canvas I never know how it will come out. This is the risk you must take. I never visualize a picture in my mind before starting to paint. On the contrary, I believe that a picture is finished only after one has completely effaced the idea that was there at the start."

This statement by a French Cubist might very well have been made by the Dutch-American Abstract Expressionist Willem de Kooning. A characteristic De Kooning (see cover) is many paintings in one: paintings that lie under the one finally seen, giving it structure and force. These earlier stages have emerged and been obliterated, leaving behind

PLATE 30: Mark Tobey, *Edge of August*, 1953. Casein on board, 48" x 28"

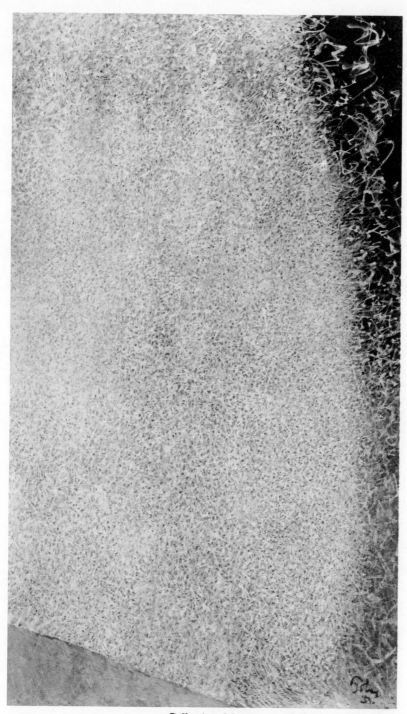

Collection, Museum of Modern Art, New York

their traces of direction and decision. As has been observed, out of one passage in a De Kooning, other painters have produced whole exhibitions.

The richness of De Kooning's procedure is partly due to the richness of his pictorial motifs, but it is also due to the unrelenting agitation of his work. Unlike Braque, De Kooning is little interested in the "rule that corrects the emotion." "Art," he has said, "never seems to make me peaceful or pure. I always seem to be wrapped in the melodrama of vulgarity. I do not think of inside or outside—or of art in general—as a situation of comfort . . . Some painters, including myself . . . have found that painting—any kind of painting, any style of painting, to be painting at all, in fact—is a way of living today, a style of living . . ."

Here lies a partial justification for referring to these Abstract Expressionists as "action painters." With these artists that "style of living" has a sense of involvement and of questioning, a sense which makes a given painting not so much an object as a sort of battlefield on which the evidence of actions and decisions remains and touches us immediately in our own lives.

Hans Hofmann once warned: "To worship the product and ignore its development leads to dilettantism and reaction." By this criterion, "objective" painting today is reactionary, for simple depiction is no longer a way of arriving at meaning. Likewise, a non-objective painting which rests at being a beautiful finished object without conveying the quality of its growth and development, lacks something vital.

The idea of "action" in contemporary painting implies not only gesture and process, but suggests also a vehemence, even an aggressiveness, characteristic of modern American society. Kline and De Kooning cut and slash, and many artists virtually attack their canvases, much as a pianist today may be described as "attacking" Haydn.

Abstract Expressionist painting is not the only style that counts today; neither is it the end of art history. But it does represent the richest painting of the past quarter century; it exhibits the greatest range and depth and has already established the groundwork for coming generations.

In Abstract Expressionism may be found not only the viable residue of the major previous styles of the twentieth century—Cubism and abstract art, Expressionism and Surrealism—but also the central subjects for the art of our time. These might, for convenience of argument, be reduced to four components: first, the exploitation of the primary aesthetic factors—that is, lines, shapes, colors and pigments—for their own tangible and suggestive powers; second, the experiencing of a work of art as a process rather than a product; third, the direct evocation of the artist's inner life in such a way that the meaning becomes universally human; fourth, the deobjectification of forms and their immersion in the forces of universal nature.

This last may vary from the Milky Ways soaring through Jackson Pollock's vast canvases to the delicate *Edge of August* (Plate 30) of Mark Tobey. Here the edge of August seems inseparable from the edge of a solar body, and a kind of solar energy seems to precipitate the energy of the painting. Likewise, this art may range from the contemplation of the inner meaning of a piece of bark to that vast sense, anticipated by Wordsworth, of "moving about in worlds not realized."

This "expressionist" aspect of Abstract Expressionism is therefore capable of ranging from the intimate to the universal, and embodies some of the most meaningful experiences of our time. Depth psychology, existentialism and the solipsism of modern man's experience of his world combine with art as art and art as process, and these in turn, with nature seen as at once tangible and ineffable.

Yet this art is always abstract, and it is always painting (in contrast to Pop and Op and other forms of non-painting). It is to be seen and felt for what lies specifically within it, regardless of metaphysical, spiritual or scientific implications. One must learn its language, and the language

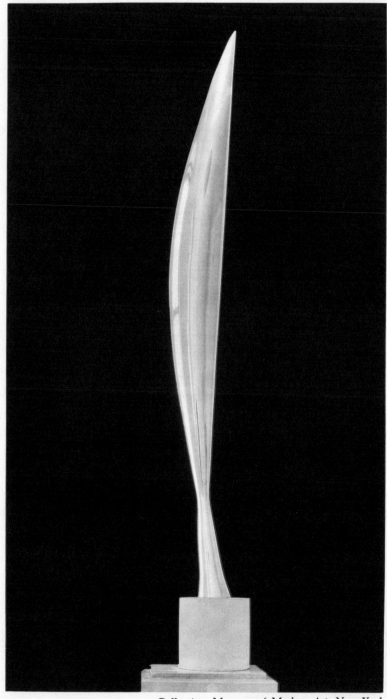

Collection, Museum of Modern Art, New York
PLATE 31: Constantin Brancusi, *Bird in Space*, 1919. Bronze, 54″ high

PLATE 32: Fritz Bultman, Vase of Winds II, 1961–62. Bronze, 59½″ high

Collection of the Whitney Museum of American Art, New York

can be understood only through persistent and sympathetic looking and feeling. The person who cannot, in time, come to feel the vitality and meaning of abstract art is like the person who can hear in a song only the words and not the music.

Relatively little space in this book has been given to sculpture, as compared to painting. The reason is simple: during the past two centuries, painting has been by far the richest and most significant of the visual arts which work in images, and almost always it has been the leader as well. Therefore, if one grasps the nature of modern painting, he should have a little less difficulty with modern sculpture.

In stressing the leadership of painting during the modern age, I am not going so far as to agree with that sometimes miraculous art critic, Baudelaire, who felt that in all its vital periods sculpture was the handmaiden to another art. While this is true today and has often been true in the past (in the late Middle Ages, for example), it was certainly not true of the Egyptian sculpture after the age of the Pyramids, or of Classical Greece, or of central Italy from Donatello to Michelangelo. And perhaps it is inappropriate, even impertinent, to see in the strength and independence of the sculpture of Rodin, Brancusi, Henry Moore or David Smith nothing but appendages to or derivations from painting.

Still, it is hardly coincidental that so much of the best modern sculpture has been produced by painters themselves. In the nineteenth century much of the best sculpture, even if fragmentary, was produced by Géricault, Daumier, Degas, Renoir and Gauguin. In the twentieth century, important sculpture—often as important and fertile as that produced by the professional sculptors—has come from the hands of such painters as Picasso, Braque, Matisse, Modigliani, Max Ernst, Paul Nash, Kurt Schwitters, Giacomo Balla, Joan Miró, Dubuffet, Léger, Asger Jorn, Karel Appel, Barnett Newman, Fritz Bultman, Nicholas Carone, Jacques Brown, Alphonso Ossorio or Robert Rauschenberg, to name only a few.

At the same time, professional sculptors from Rodin to the present have returned sculpture to an ambitiousness and vitality perhaps unequaled since the seventeenth century. Much of the richer sculpture of the seventeenth and eighteenth centuries is to be found in architectural decoration, as revived in the still underrated designs of late-nineteenth-century architects, such as Antonio Gaudi, Hector Guimard, Victor Horta or Louis Sullivan (Plate 29). In our time, however, most architecture has been non-decorative, and sculpture can boast of having returned to its own as a full-scale figurative art form.

The use of "figurative" here refers to the creation of original configurations (for their own sake, as opposed to architecture), not to the use of the figure as such. While sculpture has always been of all arts the most dedicated to the exploitation of the figure, and while the figure has been more persistent in modern sculpture than in painting, still the most promising modern sculpture is abstract.

The situation in sculpture is categorically different today from what it was in the Renaissance. The Renaissance and Baroque tradition focused so completely on the figure that it was used to convey almost every meaning. Muses and mountains, oceans and river gods, wars and rapes, nymphs and passions, all became human figures. This metaphor was maintained as late as Rodin and Maillol, though with Rodin the static figure tended to become transformed into flowing pieces and forces, and with Maillol it was apparently more of a limitation than the vital vocabulary which it had been for Bernini.

With Brancusi, Henry Moore and modern sculpture on the whole, the metaphor of the human figure has been dropped in favor of an abstract vocabulary of metaphorical material and form, a vocabulary as infinite as the range of twentieth-century materials from the natural to the synthetic, and at once general and precise. Ever since Marcel Duchamp revealed the value of investigating every "thing" as a potential source of sculptural form, the found object has played a role in sculpture commensurate with that of collage in painting.

Comparable to Mondrian in his attempt to purify the elements of art and to simplify structure to the utmost is Constantin Brancusi, one of the seminal sculptors of the twentieth century. Despite the purity of his forms, there are indispensable associative qualities. In a work such as *Bird in Space* (Plate 31), a sense of soaring, even an intimation of jet propulsion, is achieved *within* the form, and not by a reference to surroundings. At the same time the treatment of the metal expresses a joy in the qualities of surface and substance, as well as contributing to the sensation of speed and flow.

In other works Brancusi exploits and purifies the inherent qualities of wood or stone, but never simply for their own sake, always in the service of feelings involved in an image or an object. To put it another way, unlike a number of other modern sculptors, Brancusi does not elicit a sense of the native quality in a material as being exciting in itself alone; this excitement is always infused with pertinent emotion and embodied in significant form.

And this form, despite its abstraction and simplification, is usually responsive to the secret workings of nature. One might say of Brancusi's work as the painter-sculptor Hans Arp said of his own, that it invoked the "natural process of condensation, hardening, coagulating, thickening, growing together." Also, as with Mondrian, the perfection and purity of Brancusi's form, though final, is never closed: instead, it opens outward with a characteristically twentieth-century expansiveness.

It would take another volume to do any sort of justice to the breadth of modern sculpture, not to mention the hard-won steps necessary to relinquish the old language and establish the new. Here there is room to mention only a few distinctive styles and personalities. The refined forms of Brancusi were pursued in a dangerously mechanical way by the Constructivists (notably Naum Gabo and Antoine Pevsner). The purism which with Brancusi always acted to refine and articulate ideas

Courtesy of Marlborough-Gerson Gallery, New York. Estate of David Smith

PLATE 33: David Smith, left: *Cubi XIX*, 1963, 9′5⅛″; center: *Cubi XVII*, 1963, 8′11¾″; right: *Cubi XVIII*, 1964, 9′7¾″. Stainless steel

incarnate in the subject and the material has, with many subsequent sculptors in that tradition, become a limitation.

Some of the most interesting of modern sculpture is vitally involved with a sense of environment. This may take the form of the box worlds of Joseph Cornell or Louise Nevelson; it may involve correlations between paintings and sculptures; or it may involve a specific interaction with space. In the sculpture of Seymour Lipton or Herbert Ferber, this spatial activity seems to be working *into* the form; in the sculpture of Alexander Calder or David Smith (Plate 33), the form might be seen as working *out* into space. With Smith this expansive power can in a given context "fill" scores of cubic yards. Calder is most famous for his "mobiles"; yet their greatest significance may lie in a revelation, to sculptor and spectator alike, of new possibilities of interactions of form and space, of statics in relation to dynamics, of felt or implicit movement in stable sculpture. Interesting in this connection are recent explorations of machinelike dynamics, sometimes emerging in vital push-and-pull compositions, such as those by Joseph Konzal or James Wines.

Still the most promising area for contemporary sculpture seems to lie in what I would call organic form. The best work of Lipton, Ferber or Bultman creates form which is basic to sculpture in being substantial and tangible but at the same time realizes itself as force and energy. With Bultman (Plate 32) the form responds to sensations of growth and intuitions of metamorphosis; the form expands sympathetically into its environment; it is ceaselessly tentative yet inherently authoritative. Different views of the same piece are a further contribution of the art of photography toward the apprehension of the art of sculpture.

Might we speculate that because of its nature content, much contemporary painting will come to be displayed in outdoor settings? Much modern sculpture is at its most effective under an open sky; Henry Moore's monumental figures are not only mountainlike in their qualities of piling, rolling and eroding, but look most striking against a back-ground of hills. And David Smith's brisk and rugged metalwork is nowhere more impressive and meaningful than arrayed on that long hillside overlooking Lake George (Plate 33).

Wood, stone and metal can be exposed to the open air, and indeed, may look better for being weathered, but what about paint and canvas? How can they be exhibited outdoors and still be protected from the elements? Edvard Munch provided one solution. The critic J.P. Hodin recalls that in a visit to the artist's home in 1938, he was shown an open-air studio that Munch called "my invention." Hodin recounts:* "We came to a brown wooden partition and Munch let us through. A square enclosed room with a narrow strip of roof all around it but open to the sky in the center . . . He used this 'invention' in summer and winter, and the paintings hung there year in, year out, in wind and weather. He could come and look at them in different lights and at different times of the day or year and see them as if they were the work of another." Such an arrangement, in any of its variations, might be tried in galleries and museums as well as in the artist's studio.

* *The Dilemma of Being Modern*, New York, n.d., p. 32.

IX | THE PRESENT STATE OF ART

While abstract art is still very much alive, in recent years certain other developments have caught popular attention: a new role of the figure in abstract painting and even a certain amount of figure painting in itself; a resurgence of "hard edge" painting (see Plate 37), sometimes in the form of "Optical" art; and the emergence of a new realistic or "Pop" art.

Though it is a new genre, Pop art has a very close ancestor in Dada. The similarity in names is accidental, and neither has anything at all to do with "father." Dada means "hobbyhorse" in French, both literally and as an *idée fixe*, while Pop is short for "popular." Dada and Pop originated in reaction to the hyperseriousness, highly aesthetic focus and acute anxieties characteristic of analytic Cubism in the first instance and Abstract Expressionism in the second. Both schools sought a release from formality—a comic relief—and expressed an attitude that negated art. There are, however, important differences. One might say that Dada is more anti-art (i.e., Dali and his *Mona Lisa's Moustache*), whereas Pop is simply non-art. Moreover, Dada sounds a note of civilized despair, whereas Pop tends to be culturally callous and to surrender to the machine.

Most of the qualities which make Abstract Expressionism intense and difficult are rejected by Pop art: painting as process, painting as structured surface, painting as an incessant conflict between the artist and the work, painting as a phenomenon developing its own subjects, art as metamorphosis of the object, as a gesture of life, as deadly issue—all these conditions and conflicts are overturned or ignored. In place of the challenge, the search, the question, Pop provides the prepackaged product and flirts with the cliché.

To speak of Abstract Expressionism as embodying deadly issues may sound like strong wording; yet this struggle has been attested to by artists themselves. Clyfford Still has warned: "Let no man undervalue the implications of this work, or its power for life, or for death, if it is misused."

This remark could be subjected to ridicule if taken in the most literal sense. Clearly, the artist is referring to a spiritual problem, and the mere presence of such a problem is the issue here. Even so, it is interesting to take note of Vasari's story about Raphael, who sent a painting (which was to be placed on an altar) to the painter Francia, with a letter asking him "to repair any scratch that might be found on the painting, and further requested that, if he perceived any defect, he would as a friend, correct it for him. Francia caused the picture, with the greatest joy, to be taken into a good light, and had it removed from its case. But such was the astonishment it caused him, and so great was his admiration for it that, perceiving his own error and the foolish presumption with which he had weakly believed in his own superiority, he took it deeply to heart, and falling ill with his grief, in a very short time he died of its effects."

No such issues, no such feelings, inform Pop art; quite the contrary, its aim is to eschew issue, to relax tension, to turn away from the difficult and the unfamiliar toward that which appears so easy that perhaps only an artist would think of it (like casting two beer cans in bronze), or to that which is so familiar that perhaps only a poet could see it in a novel way. Where the abstract artist is totally involved, the Pop artist plays the role of voyeur.

The content of Pop art may be a gigantic sculptured hamburger, or a variation on that hamburger (Plate 34), a blown-up panel from a comic strip, a life-sized plaster cast of a woman on a bicycle, a varied reproduction of the American flag, a collage combining painting and sculpture (this is seldom found in serious art), a painting of row on row of Campbell soup cans, a montage of images of Marilyn Monroe. This last idea was derived from the serious art of De Kooning; once again a revolution has its source in the order against which it revolts. From abstract art Pop borrows several broad characteristics: the tendency toward large size, the tough and vigorous approach, and the interest in shock value. But the shock value in Pop does not touch profound metaphysical anxiety (as in De Kooning) or explore the abyss of modern life (as with Motherwell)—rather, it is the shock of the familiar and absurd. A little change in an ordinary object, an unexpected context— and the viewer is amused, even relieved. Abstract Expressionism had carried art to a dangerous tension. Pop art is really not so much a reaction against this as a suspension of hyperserious activity. According to the non-Pop, non-abstract painter Fairfield Porter, "Pop art is an abortive attempt to show that painting today, especially that of the maturing *avant-garde,* is entirely in the hands of stuffed shirts."

On the whole, Pop artists disclaim any attempt at social comment. What interests them is how some of the commonest elements of daily life may look when they are blown up out of size, repeated beyond the point of monotony—or even seen for the elements of art that they may contain. Some of these artists—Claus Oldenberg, for instance—employ a deliberate crudeness that denies "artiness"; others, like James Rosenquist, employ a deliberate commercial slickness which denies art as a problematic process.

Abstract Expressionism developed the brush stroke to an unprecedented degree as an essential aesthetic element. Pop art rarely shows a brush stroke. Abstract Expressionism is concerned with dimensions of space and time; Pop art makes a joke of space and seeks to congeal the moment. It might be called Instant Art, with all the connotations of the easy, the second-rate, the momentary. Again, this is part of the urge for relief.

Robert Indiana has said of Pop: "It walks young for the moment without the weight of 4000 years of art history on its shoulders." No art can do this for long, especially in an age that is intensely aware of history. (Compare Cézanne's view: "One does not substitute oneself for the past; one merely adds a new link to the chain.") But like aspirin, Pop's brightly self-advertising presentations can bring temporary relief.

It is often noted that Pop rejects the *abstract*ness of modern art and turns to a "new objectivity." But it is equally significant that Pop rejects *expressionism,* turning instead to decoration. In doing so, it suggests the probability that advertising is the decorative art of our time.

In a Gothic town not the cathedral only but houses, shops and walls were covered with brightly colored carvings or painted images. In the eighteenth century, Versailles embellished its architecture and landscap-

PLATE 34: Mel Ramos, Vernaburger, 1965. Oil on canvas, 50″ x 60″

ing with gaily painted figures and ornaments. It is often said by city planners and the like that only modern urban life has created buildings without ornament, streets without statues, an environment without decorative art. But is this entirely true? The modern city is filled with visual activity. The neon sign, the billboard, the traffic light, the poster, the marquee, the subway entrance, even the skywriting above, proclaim a city keyed to physical and nervous activity, pronounce the rhythm of its functions and call upon native and visitor to avail themselves of its goods and ills. Here is the decorative art of modern life—blatant, restless, boundless and ever changing. It antagonizes and stimulates, exhausts and excites.

Pop art did not discover this world; many artists from Toulouse-Lautrec to Picasso, from Joseph Stella to Stuart Davis, and in some respects the Futurists, have responded to the same scene or made their art from its motifs. But Pop artists have gone further in that they make this scene the *total* content of their art. In doing so, they tend to minimize the distinction between original objects and their own re-creation of them.

Certain abstract painters had apprenticeships as house painters; certain Pop artists began as sign painters. Neither fact has overwhelming significance in the history of art, but there is at least something symbolic here. The house painter responded to the scale of his activity and to the activity of painting. The sign painter made *signs*. In a commercial sign the art of painting consists of little more than control, and the purpose of the activity is not to create a live surface, but to signal to an audience. Pop art flirts with communication.

In this respect also, Pop reverts to a literary art. Unlike Surrealism, which was literary in origin, Pop is chiefly visual; its literary aspect lies rather in its literalness. There have been tedious debates as to whether Pop transforms, interprets, represents or merely presents. Surely even in the recasting of an ale can, the object is transformed; whether the result is a transcending experience is quite another question. For another example, a painting by Roy Lichtenstein which depicts a panel from a comic strip is not only highly suggestive, but transforms the object in size and technique. The result is unquestionably a new experience, but it may be questionable whether it is a profound one.

In fairness, its practitioners usually do not claim it to be. Pop is the first art since Dada that is meant to be laughed at. So is the original comic strip, but one might be tempted to cite Don Herald's ancient comment that "comic strip artists do not make good husbands, and God knows they do not make good comic strips." Lichtenstein's paintings are often funnier than the so-called comics.

On the other hand, an artist like Larry Rivers (antedating the Pop artists but really belonging with them), with such paintings as *Washington Crossing the Delaware* and other take-offs, seems like the Grant Wood of our day, although there is little in Rivers even as moderately funny as Wood's *Daughters of Revolution* or *American Gothic*.

Whether Pop comic strips, heroic-sized hamburgers and washstands amount to art is dubious. But this is less important than the fact that Pop, like Dada, is by its own avowal anti- or non-art. Emerging on the one hand from areas outside the visual arts such as the "happening," and on the other hand from such commercially "artistic" influences as advertising, window display or schools of design, Pop can hardly take itself any more seriously than the "fine art" it repudiates.

Although its works are sometimes of distinct quality and often of genuine shock value, Pop could not be defended as a very ambitious art. It does not transform its own materials; it does not explore the self or the inner life; and it does not perform the function to which Sir Herbert Read referred when he observed that art should lead the public, not follow it.

Still, this is not to say that Pop art cannot play a healthy or even a significant role. Just as in politics, in the history of art there are moments when there is a real emotional need for relief, for a *détente*. The relaxed state of Pop art has, at least momentarily, abated the complex tensions of abstract art. It has not really interfered with the continuation of abstract art by its ablest practitioners, but it has exposed the drifters who adopt whatever approach is popularly successful. In effect, it has been a cleansing influence in abstract art.

But Pop has also set craft against art, no-think against thought. When asked, What do you think about Pop art? one may be tempted to reply, I don't think about it. And perhaps one need not try to say too much either, though surely Pop is easier to talk about than Cubism or Abstract Expressionism. For Pop really introduces and describes itself. It is an art of young people, bent on displaying their new-won professional skill or on releasing a kind of college humor. It is given to youthfully simple solutions. Pop is refreshing. Pop is here to stay, though not for long. While of dubious stature as art, it should contribute something to the arts of the future.

Both Pop and Op—whatever their claims to artistic status—might be more clearly referred to as "minimal art." That is to say, they are vital enough to attract the momentary concern of critics and dealers; yet they occupy no real position in the mainstream of modern painting. One might very well say of Op art what the critic George Dennison proposed of Pop, that "certain kinds of sophisticates make up the audience of Pop. If there is a choice between emotion and titillation they'll choose the latter . . ." Pop and Op come very close to being fashions. Dress designers have bought designs from leading Op artists, and Pop is already having a marked influence in the field of advertising, thus making an appropriate return to the source from which it sprang.

To the extent that they approach fine art, as opposed to fashion or display, Pop and Op tend to be rationalizing arts. Where Pop rationalizes about subject matter, finding a variety of images in tabloids or commercial life, Op rationalizes about visual effects (Plate 35). In this

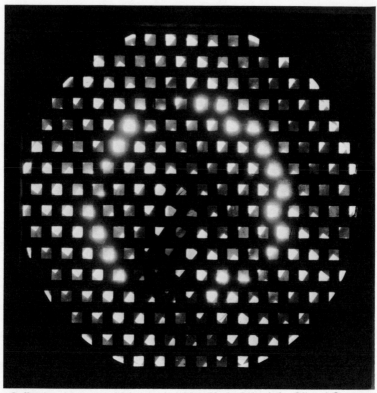

Collection, Museum of Modern Art, New York. Gift of the Olivetti Company of Italy

PLATE 35: Grazia Varisco, *Dynamic Lattice A*, 1962. Plexiglass, card-board lattices, with light and motor, in wooden box, 20¼" x 20¼" x 5⅞"

it approaches optical experiments performed by scientists and technicians. In fact, a recent exhibition of Op art included *moiré* patterns (the effect of placing a lens over an image) silk-screened on plexiglass by Dr. Gerald Oster, a scientist rather than an artist. The significant resemblance of these patterns to a number of Op paintings provides a strong contrast with Impressionism, which for all its optical effects was always an art in that its primary concern was with the expressive poetry of painting.

As with Pop art, Op shows a considerable variety in both its devices and its practitioners. Among the favored effects in Op paintings are the play of the after-image, the manipulation of planes which advance and recede simultaneously, the interaction of the stable and the unstable (for example, a picture that appears to be composed of curves, both in two and three dimensions, yet actually consists in nothing but straight lines), the *moiré* effect referred to above, or the visually intriguing and ungraspable sensations of wave patterns that come and go within themselves, suggesting the corona of the sun (as in the bull's eyes of Ellsworth Kelly and others) or effects like a scintilla, a penumbra or an aureole.

Little of this is new to painting. The idea of an art whose subject matter is based on optical effects goes back at least to Impressionism, and it was further developed in Neo-Impressionism. Already in 1890 Seurat was writing of his interest in a *peinture optique*. The Bauhaus movement of the 1920's and thirties, with its interest in the relationships between design and optical effects, is the specific source of much of contemporary art. Pollock's development of the painting as an over-all field of visual activity is still another major ingredient. Mondrian's development of illusory interstices where lines cross in his mature paintings is also relevant. His last works, *Broadway Boogie Woogie* and *Victory Boogie Woogie*, deliberately employed retinal vibrations as a key part of the visual experience. One could also point to specific stylistic sources, such as the evident origin of Jasper Johns' *Large Black Five* (1960) in Charles Demuth's *I Saw the Figure Five in Gold* (1928). Not least, it should be remembered that the first real Op artists—men like Josef Albers, Auguste Herbin or Victor de Vasarely—are all of an earlier generation.

Experimentation in color effects can be traced back to the dazzling vibrations and whirling motions of late Roman mosaics or even more ancient examples. In our own time, Ad Reinhart in some of his early work dealt with color jumps, and it would be no exaggeration to say that most painters have toyed with and found discomfort in the vibration of juxtaposed complementary colors, especially when they are at the same value—and that most painters have rejected such devices. None of the individual effects in Op art is new; what marks the style is the full and exclusive exploitation of certain effects mainly for their own sake.

Considering its sources outside art, it is impossible to dissociate the emergence of Op from academic design projects, textbook exercises, laboratory experiments on the operation of light, and advertising techniques (primarily for form, whereas it is the content that chiefly interests Pop), or even the visual effects of the television tube and screen. All of these pull Op dangerously close to the applied rather than the creative arts.

This is not to say that all Op art is not art. In *Night on Cold Mountain* (Plate 36) by Larry Poons, to take a promising example, the vibration of blue dots in and against an orange field is caused by the particular quality of the complementary colors and by a fluctuation of after-images. But the painting is not limited to these visual effects. For one thing, there is the beguiling effect of the precise placement of the dots against faint grid lines. Searching out their spatial groupings and interactions, one feels a kind of order that can almost—if not quite—be grasped. The procedure resembles musical notation; yet the effect is suggestive of groupings of stars and planets. Thus, there is a further fluctuation between the sense that these dots are ordered by the mind of man and the intimation of some cosmic plan. And this in turn may raise the question of plan in the cosmos—a question as to whether the forms of constellations and galaxies were derived from rhythmic forces or from accident.

In other words, in such a painting as this there is a play between the ideas of formal and random location. Again this sense of the random organization of a field can be traced at least to Impressionism, although in a good Monet (Color Plate 1), for example, the apparently random composition is infused with an almost unconscious but powerful structuring of compositional elements. In the Poons the relationship between the formal and the random has been made the chief subject of the picture.

In addition, a new approach to the relationship between the formal and the random may be suggested here. As L.L. Whyte has noted with enthusiasm, theoretical scientists have recently become interested in a new approach to the problems of form, one which seeks to remove older distinctions between order and disorder, symmetry and asymmetry, structure and randomness. So far these attempts to provide a new apparatus for comprehending all levels of form and structure, from proton to galaxy, have produced only tentative propositions, but it is conceivable that painting, which in the West has long pursued courses parallel to those of science and philosophy, may come up with some intuitions and apprehensions of its own.

The question remains, Is the Poons painting a work of art? Neither optical effects nor metaphysical implications can produce art of themselves. However, there is something gratifying in the relationships between color and space in this painting, and the dots twinkle in their firmament with a precocious sense of life.

For Op art on the whole, the conclusion is more dismal. Some critics propose that even if most Op is not art, at least it has re-emphasized visual experience, which after all, it is claimed, is the primary function of art. This sounds logical. Yet if one were to consult artists from Goethe and Wordsworth to Constable and Corot, to Picasso, Kandinsky and Kline, one would find unequivocal testimony that the primary value of art is not visual, but emotional.

To this value, painting will surely return; meanwhile, painting is still going on. Just as an earlier generation survived Dada and Bauhaus, and as modern art will survive Pop and Op, so in the future our children will survive momentary reactions to the more difficult and serious forms of painting. These reactions can be refreshing, but they are bound to be sporadic.

What of the present and immediate future? There seems little left now for these diversionary forms except perhaps "painting by the numbers" or sheer pornography. The latter has always been a sideline of art, but it seems less likely to become popular because it is not as acceptable as pornography in print. Painting by the numbers, of which some examples are currently being exhibited, seems another variety of the Pop-Op syndrome—that is, it avoids anything truly original, but tries instead to find something to copy that no one has copied before.

As for the more virulent forms of Op art, ironically both artist and public feel they must commit themselves to an art that actually hurts when you look at it.

Two more serious trends of the moment, as mentioned earlier, are a resurgence of "hard edge" painting and re-emergence of both figure painting in itself, and the use of the figure within abstract paintings.

Certain hard-edge painters, such as Ellsworth Kelly or Myron Stout (Plate 37), have been pursuing their own course for years. Kelly's large paintings have some of the shock and decorative impact of Pop, along with an overt simplicity of form and structure. Stout's paintings are smaller, and though simple in their elements, are highly complex in execution. With only a black and a white form but elaborating on the

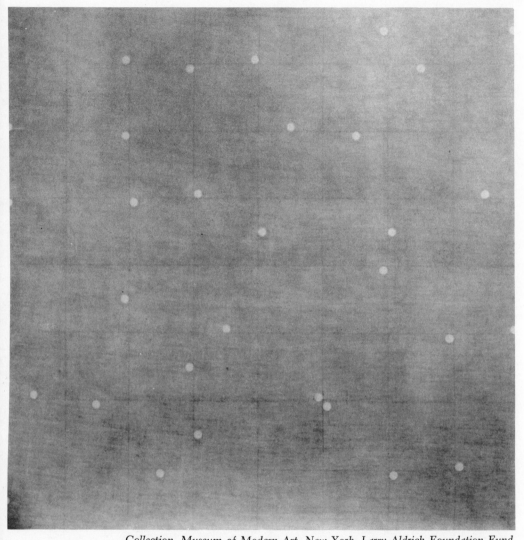

Collection, Museum of Modern Art, New York. Larry Aldrich Foundation Fund
PLATE 36: Larry Poons, *Night on Cold Mountain*, 1962. Polymer and dye on canvas, 80″ x 80″

precise qualities of surface and finish, his pictures produce a vibration of positive and negative in which black and white play interchanging roles. Directions are strongly implied and at the same time just as surely countered, so that the result is a feeling of suspension. Edges are of the utmost importance in establishing these effects, and the artist has been known to rework a single painting for years, until all the experiences of up and down, left and right, in and out or back and forth attain a satisfactory equilibrium. Yet this equilibrium of varying forces and factors would count for little if the picture did not begin and end with a unified and telling image.

The re-emergence of the figure in the work of a number of painters, among them Lester Johnson and Tony Vevers (Color Plate 9), is not a reaction against abstract painting in the way that Pop was. For this new figure painting is essentially abstract; the human image is still anonymous and inseparable from its field, and the execution is still very much painting. The blunt strength and vigorous impasto of Johnson's art has a counterpart in the delighted lyricism and sensuous grace of Vevers, a painter who reminds us that the external light of nature and its poetic power to elicit mood can still be a viable source of art in the second half of the twentieth century. Vevers's pictures often contain literal elements, but these do not make his art easy to define. At its best, it might remind us of what Ingres said about Corot, that "this devil of a fellow gets into his figures something that the specialists have never been able to put into theirs."

The range of relationships between abstract and figurative elements among contemporary painters is considerable and promising. Edward Corbett continues to paint pictures that appear abstract but are largely landscape in feeling, tone and experience; they are deceptively decorative, often surprisingly resonant, and whether joyous or tragic, always true. Sherman Drexler paints the figure purely but in terms emerging out of abstract art. His anonymous but personal figures are suspended spatially in a way that adds suspense to their sensuality—and keeps them from ever being lonely. Stephen Pace, after a long experience in robust abstract painting, now often paints figures in a dialogue with abstracted yet evocative settings.

Women painters, who have played a livelier role in the art of the last twenty years than in any other time since the eighteenth century, are often involved in a tension between the associations of the image and the pure abstraction. Paintings of Helen Frankenthaler or Joan Mitchell may become, on living with them, less abstract than they first appear. Unusually effective integrations of abstract thinking with the meaningfulness of figure and gesture may be found in the work of Elizabeth Holliday (Color Plate 10), whose large, strong canvases sweep all elements into a complete and compelling counterpoint. The abstractly drawn but expressively conceived figures of Linda Lindeberg (Plate 38) suggest forms ranging from forest growth to the eloquent gestures of Daumier's clowns.

Each of these artists seems to think particularly, even if not exclusively, in terms of black and white, and it might be to the point to question the common assumption that women, as artists, tend to be colorists.

A recent trend, often predicted and occasionally practiced, is a merging of painting and sculpture, or vice versa—for no particular reason, it seems, other than to open up another possibility in art. With an artist such as Sven Lukin, for example, the results of his brilliantly colored, broad three-dimensional surfaces are striking, and sometimes this further "projects" a color. Nevertheless, his work actually seems most interesting when it is nearest to being two-dimensional: in such pieces there is more tension between colors and planes; in short, the work appears less flat when it is more flat. Modern painting has generally been most

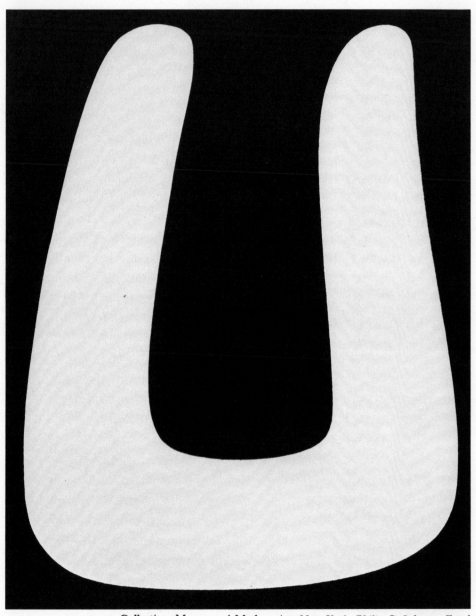

PLATE 37: Myron Stout, Number 3, 1954. Oil on canvas, 20⅛″ x 16″

meaningful when most painterly, just as sculpture has been most effective when most sculptural. Recent attempts to combine the two now disparate disciplines—other than in hanging them together, which can be very rich—seem doomed to self-limitation.

The same fate will, I suspect, befall most of the currently popular "kinetic" and "environmental" art. The kinetic (moving) contraptions of Jean Tinguely and other less interesting artists do not always compare favorably with the actual world of machines, many of which produce their own beauty out of the organic necessities of economy, rhythm or precision. (Consider Plate 35.)

As with Optical art, in these areas, science and art come close. A mechanism constructed by an American nuclear physicist in which rich color effects are conditioned directly by the intensities and vibrations of music played into it is more interesting as an idea than as an aesthetic object. These color effects, incidentally, are kept random, rather than being predictable, through the interference of certain wheels; similarly, the bouncing ping-pong balls and comparable moving objects popular in kinetic art insist on randomness—a principle that essentially unites such different modern artists as Monet and Picasso, or Mondrian and Pollock.

Or in a box by Julio Le Parc where changing lights move through and across corrugated surfaces, one may be reminded of certain effects of analytic Cubism. Artistically these kinetic works can hardly compare with the best of modern painting; nevertheless, there must be a distinction between those which are merely exercises, no matter how interesting, and those which transcend their immediate effect and create a new one that can be called art. To my taste, some of the most interesting kinetic works are liquids in tubes or plaques, which operate randomly yet rhythmically when they are agitated or their position is changed. Is this art?

The same question could be asked of much of the current environmental painting and sculpture. It may be fascinating in itself, it may stimulate, challenge or comment—but its content is attributable to the vagaries of society, its form to those of display.

Like Pop and Op, experiments in kinetics and environment stand apart from the main interests of modern art, which, broadly speaking, have lain in "pure" painting or sculpture. The twentieth century in particular has turned to internal experience, as well as to private and personal imagery; for example the incidence of the eye, or of the inner eye, as an image in painting has been impressive since Redon.

In comparing the general "outward" orientation of the nineteenth century with the inward impulse of the twentieth, it would be inappropriate to say that one or the other is preferable: it is simply that in a given epoch one tends to be more meaningful. But artists as individuals tend toward the one type of experience or the other as a matter of innate temperament.

As Henry Moore has said, "Not to like abstract qualities or not to like reality is to misunderstand what sculpture and art are about. Some artists are more visual, or get more excitement from nature in front of them . . . other people do it from their insides . . ." The entire history of art could be seen in terms of the interplay of cultural context and individual bent. In the Middle Ages religion fostered almost all art; yet it was not infrequent for an artist of non-religious spirit to operate true to his own nature, at the same time contributing something meaningful to the cultural scheme.

In the twentieth century—which if not actually anti-religious is largely unreligious—it is still possible for a truly devout temperament such as Rouault's to make art with truth and passion. Nevertheless, Rouault could not employ the older religious iconography in literal form. During the Middle Ages those iconographic images contained meaning by their very presence, just as did figures and objects during the Renaissance. The twentieth century must express its most vital experience in anonymous imagery, in fields of force and flux rather than in

static objects, and in internally rather than externally inspired sensations; nevertheless, within these general restrictions the possible variations are as many as the incidence of individual genius.

In an interview with Pierre Bonnard, recorded in 1943 by Angele Lamotte, the artist said, "All around me I see interesting things, but in
order for me to want to paint them they must have a personal attraction
—beauty—what one really might call the beautiful. I paint trying not to
lose the immediate conception; I am weak—if I let myself go, as with
the bouquet of roses, at the end of a moment I have lost my original
vision and I no longer know where (or how) to proceed."

In the course of the same interview Lamotte asked, "But then you
never work from nature, from the motif?"

Bonnard: "Yes, but then I leave it alone, I bring it under control—I
return after a while but I do not allow myself to be absorbed by the
object itself . . . I do everything in my studio [contrast nineteenth-
century nature painting from Constable to Cézanne]. In a word a
conflict is produced between the initial conception . . . and the
changeable, varied world of the object, of the motif . . . The painters
who are able to approach the subject directly are very rare . . ." (Bonnard then cited Titian and Cézanne as examples of the direct approach.)

For all his native instinct to work in response to the outside object,
Bonnard notes that he will not allow himself to be absorbed by it. He
stresses the conflict between the initial conception and the final realization and in general betrays an entirely twentieth-century approach to the
problem of painting.

The general direction of modern art has been toward difficult styles,
abstract in conception and more analogous to music than to literature. If
historical trends mean anything at all, it would be safe to say that
abstract art is here to stay—surely it is very much alive at present.

Collection of the Artist. Photo: Charles Uht

PLATE 38: Linda Lindeberg, *Two Figures*, 1959. Ink on paper, 18″ x 24″

Purged by Pop and Op, purified by its own practitioners, this art seems likely to pursue steady goals which go back specifically for a quarter of a century and implicitly for much longer.

The figure and the object will always recur in art. They always have, and are among our most basic experiences. "Hard edge" and other simplified styles will always emerge when art has grown too complex, and "Pop" or other "easy to make" styles will intrude when the strain of self-imposed difficulties has become unendurable. But it seems inevitable that the more challenging aspects of abstract art will continue to hold the center of the stage in a modern world.

One reason for this is that ours is an open age and our society—when healthiest—is an open one. In art this openness refers both to the intense variety of possibilities within a style and to the daring and unexpected qualities and situations it relishes. While at times this builds almost unendurable pressures, that too is a mark of our age, and it is only by meeting these pressures that we can meaningfully realize ourselves, either collectively or as individuals.

These future directions of modern art are broad, but unless they are considered, it is impossible to understand the present. Individual turning points, decisions, breakthroughs and achievements will, as always, depend upon the genius and character of the individual artist. Confronted with these individual achievements, the critic who loves art more than his own words or ideas feels humble indeed.

X | MAKING YOUR OWN DISCOVERIES

Alexander Pope had read Bolingbroke, and, not understanding him, was naturally anxious to explain him to others.
—SAMUEL JOHNSON

Aesthetics is for the artist as ornithology is for the birds.
—BARNETT NEWMAN

Often the art critic feels his is not so much a thankless task as a hopeless one. What can be said about a modern painting or sculpture? With a medieval sculpture one can discuss the symbolic implications, or with a Renaissance painting the story, but in modern art any specific message tends to be irrelevant, and criticism tends to focus on style and quality. But quality is not tangible, and perhaps in the end all we can discover about a work of art is whether it is alive or dead. And the verdict tends to be a matter of how our feelings come out. One collector of modern art has said, "There are no standards for judging any kind of art. The emotional reaction you get from looking at a picture is the thing that makes you buy it." Or as Pablo Casals once said of a piece by Bach, "I've played it hundreds of times—hundreds of times—and every time I'm so moved."

Does this mean that the critic must be content with pointing the way to certain galleries, collections or museums and let the layman grope for himself? In a way it does. In another way, one woman who was eager to learn said after a gallery talk, "I see better when I hear something." Maybe the talking in itself is a stimulant to looking—it raises the suspicion that something is going on. And perhaps the critic can suggest a few ways to go about looking at art, ways which he may have discovered himself through hit and miss.

The best way to look at a picture is to have it around for some time, much as the artist did while he was working on it, or as the Renaissance patron did by hanging works in his home. These homes being less private than those of today, art was probably more widely experienced in the Renaissance. Today one can see any number of fine paintings in museums and galleries, but not under the best circumstances. The art lover's great advantage today is photography, and no doubt in time it will be possible to make reproductions of such a quality and cost that painting can occupy as large a place in our lives as long-playing records and hi-fi sets have given to music.

But just as there is nothing like live music, so there are few visual pleasures like that of owning a live painting. How to get one depends on your income, your experience, your discernment, and no doubt a little luck. Few people who have invested in original works of art have been sorry—and this quite apart from market values.

If museums or galleries are accessible, make the most of them. But it is a mistake to see art when you feel physically tired and your senses and appreciation are dulled. Look at paintings when you are fresh and eager and can give them your best energies; the artist has done no less.

Some paintings, like Renaissance murals, are best seen from a given distance; others, like Impressionist paintings, look best at variable distances. Most modern art should be seen up close—not only because the handling of paint is important as an aesthetic element, not only for the value of spatial immersion, but also since the immediacy of experience of contemporary work calls for an immediacy of contact. And pictures, like sculptures, should be touched, though museum guards may be touchy about it.

Some pictures should be walked around in, like Pollock's; others, like De Kooning's, are more rewarding if one sits steadily in front of them. All pictures should be seen in different light—morning and afternoon, winter and summer. Even the quality, direction and strength of light on an abstract painting can be very important. Many painters have found that what they painted in Provincetown, for example, did not look at all the same in New York.

Squinting is an excellent device for getting more out of a picture: the relationships of the larger areas, forms and colors emerge more readily. Or if you are near-sighted, take off your glasses, and you will be surprised at how much and how differently you will see. When you put them back on, you will be able to grasp the details of the painting in a new context.

For example, at first glance a painting by Giorgio Cavallon (Color Plate 6) may seem like little more than patches of paint. But if you squint at the picture (which really must be seen in the original), the patches turn into color and light, the forms begin to vibrate and emerge in a peculiar life of their own, and the organic relationships between color, light and form become clear and solid. By such devices one's study and appreciation of precise values, details of execution and touch become keener, since the painting has a new and more basic frame of reference. Returning to a Cavallon again and again is to enjoy more and more the spirit that projected the painting, made it necessary and transmitted itself as an ultimate existence.

Looking at a painting should be a rich, exciting, profound and—often enough—disconcerting experience, as it was for the artist to paint it. Looking is no mere exercise. Some like to look at works of art purely for the emotion it arouses, without interference of analysis. Others like to analyze (an aesthetic pleasure in itself), to ask *why* a certain work pleases, excites or moves them. Take your choice—they can both be fun.

Works of art are just as different as one's reaction to them. Some, like Pop, are designed to produce an instantaneous response; others are of the kind Schopenhauer must have had in mind when he said, "You must treat a work of art like a great man: stand before it and wait patiently until it deigns to speak." On the whole, that art which endures is apprehended slowly. And it cannot be emphasized enough that the apprehending is above all intuitive. In the apprehending of art, it would be wise to follow what Paul Klee said about the making of it: "When intuition is joined to exact research it speeds the progress of exact research . . . One learns to look behind the façade, to grasp the root of things. One learns to recognize the undercurrents, the antecedents of the visible."

One does not expect to grasp a piece of modern music at the first listening or to understand a contemporary poem at first reading. More likely the reader will have to study the poem many times before its full meaning emerges. Even of older art, Coleridge said, "The greatest poetry is only imperfectly understood."

Yet first impressions have a place. Just as a good judge of people will size someone up right away, so an experienced judge of art will value the immediate impact of a work. But he will never be content to rely on that.

Painting is one of the slowest of art forms to discover in all its qualities, experiences and values. And painters often take longer than men in other professions to develop the fullness of their style, or as they sometimes put it, to come to any understanding of what painting is really about. Of all careers, Titian's is the most remarkable: he painted until he died of plague, around the age of ninety, and his painting had grown better and stronger. (Delacroix once remarked that if he should live to be a hundred, he would come to prefer the painting of Titian to all others.)

Painting is a reflective activity, in several senses of that word. And as Delacroix said in another context, "Painting is the trade that takes longest to learn and is the most difficult. It demands erudition like that of the composer, but it demands execution like that of the violinist." The time that goes into painting—both the individual work and the entire career—deserves in return a good deal of time, patience and effort on the part of the viewer.

And what is it that we hope to get out of all this effort? Is it that we shall discover more about a painting and about the art of painting? Partly, and these are no small matters. But there is more to be gained. Bernard Berenson has written: "We must look and look and look till we live in the painting and for a fleeting moment become identified with it . . . A good rough test is whether we feel that it is reconciling us with life." Or, one might add, with love.

Since Ortega y Gasset published his influential essay two generations ago, much has been made of the modern tendency toward a "dehumanization of art." This is a subject to be approached with caution. In the sense that modern art does not seek to idealize man or to place him at the center of the universe as the measure of all creatures, then it is true that art since the Renaissance has become increasingly dehumanized.

But if we consider that this shift in attitude toward man is not restricted to art, but is to be found in all society, and notably in science, then it is missing the point to single out art as a "dehumanizer." Indeed, in important respects the opposite is true. Delacroix once observed, "The true Rome is no longer in Rome." Perhaps we shall discover that the true humanism of our century is to be found not with the Corliss Lamonts or Huntington Hartfords, but among artists themselves—in which case it makes no difference whether they work in objective or non-objective form, whether they glorify or lacerate the human image.

For it is modern man himself who has become dehumanized. More than most men, the artist seeks for the truth within himself, rather than in external situations. Coming upon the essence of something human, the artist enables the living to share the secrets of the dead, and helps us to see where we have been, what we are doing, why we live rather than how.

It is the artist who exemplifies that most difficult and most "human" of endeavors, which might be defined with André Gide as: "Look for your own. Do not care what someone else could do as well as you . . . Care for nothing in yourself but what you feel exists nowhere else—and out of yourself create . . . the most irreplaceable of beings."

From time to time doctors and lawyers are convicted of malpractice; yet about this, the layman rarely gets excited.

All a doctor or lawyer can do to one's life is fix it or finish it; he cannot change its meaning. Perhaps this is why people get so excited about art, for and against one style or another, believing in this artist or that.

If art cannot be defined, at least we can say a little about what it does. Berenson suggested it can reconcile us to life. Partly because this is not the artist's explicit intention, art is usually more effective than preaching. The creative process is mysterious, and even artists have not been able to say much about it. Sometimes it is said that the creative process is a manifestation of the ability to relate previously unrelated things. This new relationship, or new set of relationships, constitutes a new world, which is why real art is so alarming. Many a spectator, critic, indeed artist, reacts with horror to some work which in some dim sense he perceives has challenged the world to which he has adjusted, often enough with pain. This is why people so often prefer works that simply give pleasure, that decorate, that further illuminate an environment or an experience with which they are already familiar.

There are arts for everyone, and no one should be ashamed of his enjoyment of a hunting print or of Offenbach. But it is the most serious, the most devastating art that we have sought to come to grips with in these pages. Real art seeks nothing less than to symbolize life. The Greeks found such symbolism in the posture of the human figure, Michelangelo in the figure's movement; Rembrandt found it in the sorrows of a changing face, Van Gogh in the radiating sun and the night sky; Cézanne in the instrumentation of landscape and still-life, Franz Kline in the orchestration of space, form and energy. This more serious art may indulge in niceties, or it may not. Kline and Bartók, like Rembrandt and Bach, are often full of grace.

So is Beethoven; yet to a quartet partner complaining of the difficulty of his part he once said, "Do you suppose I think of your miserable fiddle when the spirit takes possession of me?" The implication of that remark is that something larger than the artist's individual temperament transmits a vital force to which the individual artist gives a hard-won form. Apparently something of this sort has been felt by artists in all ages, quite apart from the changing role of the artist in society or the metaphysical value of art in any given time.

Partly because he feels "driven" or "possessed," it would seldom occur to the artist to try to explain the meaning in his work. In reply to a gratuitous interpretation of "Childe Roland," Robert Browning said, "Oh, no, not at all. Understand, I don't repudiate it either. I only mean I was conscious of no allegorical intention in writing it." This is the attitude of many contemporary painters. For the artist his work is a multileveled, complex and contradictory, challenging and beguiling, tedious and joyous, discouraging and demanding experience. He could hardly imagine anyone seeking in his work a quick and easy meaning. To "explain" a painting rather than to experience it through the artist's terms would be meaningless. As Franz Kline said, art "has nothing to do with knowing; it has to do with giving."

· · ·

If this is a clue about how to look, the final question must be, What is one to look at? And the answer: all kinds of things. No matter how single-minded the critic and how focused in style the artist, both include in their visual experience an astonishing range of art from all eras. Even if one grants that Rembrandt is the greatest of painters, no one would wish to spend a lifetime looking at nothing but Rembrandts. Certainly Rembrandt himself did not. Nor would one advise, as a French philosopher once did, anyone to read only the best books. It is inevitable that one will look at bad art, and sometimes this can be advantageous.

Even the criterion of "excellence" is misleading for our age. Excellence as a criterion is far more appropriate to the art and criticism of the Renaissance, where both man and his works were held to be, in theory at least, perfectible. For us perfectibility is beside the point. It is not the quality of the ideal, but the quality of the struggle—with its own grandeur—that moves and reconciles us.

Again and again people ask, Where are the Raphaels—or even the Cézannes—of the twentieth century? The answer is, they are in the sixteenth and nineteenth centuries and cannot come again. We will always get a vital experience from their work, even as we will from an Old Kingdom Egyptian statue whose original meaning can barely be surmised. These still have value and form because the residue of their styles is art, not because the style could be viable in some other time or place.

Could a composer write an Elizabethan ballad in the 1960's? Compare the force as well as the style of an ancient song like "Men of Harlech" with a modern counterpart like "Stout-Hearted Men." The old German woodcuts of the fifteenth century are simple, even superficially crude, in appearance, but has anyone since made a woodcut in this style with anything like the same innocence or conviction?

There is no more point in faulting De Kooning for not being Fra Angelico than in being annoyed at the cathedral of Chartres for not following the principles of the Parthenon. And if, quite apart from this, one is still bothered by the liberties De Kooning takes (for no one has denied that he is a superb renderer), then it may be interesting to recall how people were bothered by the liberties that Cézanne took, and Monet before him, and Delacroix before that. Even so apparently conventional a painter—and in an age unsurpassed in its appreciation of art—as Veronese was accused of this. He replied, "We painters take the same liberties as poets and madmen take." Possibly a touch of the insane is a necessary ingredient in the distillation of art—an element necessary for its preservation. Saint-Gaudens observed, "What garlic is to salad, insanity is to art," and Shakespeare of course likened "the lunatic, the lover, and the poet."

Mention of the lover recalls the "giving" of which Franz Kline spoke, for though love is many things it is always giving. Art is fear and trembling, desperation and despair, tragedy and comedy, disgust and delight, revelation and titillation, finding and losing, construction and destruction—but whatever else it is, art is an original labor of love. And this love does not reside only in the work of art; rather, it is transmitted to the viewer to become a part of his life.

To look at a variety of art not only broadens but also deepens our visual experience; in so doing, we inevitably discover the works that have longer staying power. The art of Ben Shahn or Leonard Baskin may have a quicker and easier appeal, but in time it seems to have less "content"— that is, less meaningful experience—than the paintings of Mark Rothko or Clyfford Still, which at first glance might look almost empty. Not only the depth but also the quality of such an experience counts. The superficial artists aim for and produce only poignancy; the best among our contemporaries have sounded the depths of tragedy.

This is not a matter of the specific approach of the artist. Some artists make more reference to nature than others; some artists are most excited when looking at nature, others at art, others at themselves. A few manage to encompass all three at the same time, and it is partly for this reason that such artists as Matisse and De Kooning rank among the most comprehensive of the century.

One should beware the too-easy abstract picture which simply falls into the vernacular of our time. Or the artist who "packages" some familiar object with modern trappings. He should be equally suspicious of the apparently difficult but actually easy and shallow illustration that passes for art. If your taste is for an intensely illusionistic and genuinely romantic style, you might consider, not Andrew Wyeth (whose work seldom *penetrates* nature), but Thomas Eakins, Caspar David Friedrich, or Marsden Hartley.

Still, there are many worthwhile works of art that are not necessarily of the first rank. Some artists paint essentially one picture: they find a formula, and no matter how they vary its appearance, it is still the same picture. While this limits the artist as an individual, it does not necessarily lessen the individual picture, which may well gain in felicity through being reworked. Larger artists—the Turners and Courbets, the Tworkovs and Pollocks—expose themselves to a far greater range of both success and failure. If you are thinking of buying, look at the particular work at least as much as the name of the author.

And if you really are buying, choose a work because it means something to you, something that you are unwilling to do without. The vagaries of taste cannot be countered by one man alone; instead, they should be accounted for, and unless you have money to waste there is no point in buying a name artist through lack of confidence in your own judgment or a hope that some prestige may rub off.

Dealers can be dealt with and should be: they're in business. The real artist is not in business; he is not producing a commodity. He gives what he can of the only life he has—which is no doubt why Beethoven urged that one should never drive a bargain with an artist.

.　.　.

In these pages I have talked mostly of leading artists. While this is not always in the practical interests of the reader, who might like to discover lesser talents whose works he is more likely to be able to afford, the purpose has been to point up the most serious ambitions and accomplishments of modern art.

One difficulty in this revelation lies in the fact that essentially there are two kinds of artists. This is not necessarily true of politicians or businessmen, most of whom could be rated according to a scale of ability, experience or character. But in the realms of artistic and intellectual creativity we are confronted with the simple and awesome distinction between talent and genius.

This distinction is widely recognized, though variously defined. In modern art especially, it would be tempting to equate the difference between talent and genius with the distinction between followers and leaders. In more absolute—if less helpful—terms, the distinction might be thought of as that between the essentially creative and the essentially imitative. Einstein said about Max Planck's theory: if he had not thought of it, there is no reason to suppose it would ever have been thought of.

In another sense, genius can be considered a quality given to creating problems, and talent to applying solutions. Such is the implication of a critic's observation about *Les Desmoiselles d'Avignon:* here lay the end of Picasso's talent and the beginning of his genius. *Les Desmoiselles* was a work of profound dissatisfaction. Genius is never satisfied. It does not understand rules. Rules are intended for mediocrity; genius makes its own rules. Genius is a matter of interminable internal problems and requires long periods of gestation. Talent falls at the drop of a hat; John Singer Sargent could paint all day and draw all night—for him there must have been few problems.

Much as talent applies the solutions intuited by genius, so it often "applies" itself to whatever it chooses. For genius there is little choice, only a felt imperative. "The talent of medium or lesser strength disguises itself, masquerades, intentionally does now this, now that. Genius changes from inner necessity, talent for a reason," the great critic Max Friedländer observed. Or as Georges Braque remarked, "One's style—it is in a way one's inability to do otherwise."

In a day when Pop and Op, kinetic and environmental art have stolen the limelight from more ambitious art forms, critics and historians are tempted to blame the situation on the dominance of collectors' or taste-makers' whims. Yet while these factors can have considerable effect on momentary prices and popularity, they have never had much effect on the real artist. Rembrandt and Cézanne are famous for their disdain of social pressures; though exemplary, such men are far from unique. The contemporary sculptor David Hare has remarked, "It is a classical complaint that the artist is forced into certain actions by society. The artist need not be so forced, unless it is his desire to be so for motives outside art."

In the house of art there are many—sometimes too many—mansions. But there are never too many individual works of significance. In a time when it is so often said—not only by the public, and critics and dealers, but by a distressing number of artists—that art is in a state of evaporating or disintegrating or losing direction, one might emphasize that the over-all production of our generation has been one of the richest of modern times.

Non-art abounds, but it has never displaced painting—it has merely caught the spotlight. Painting is still here, going on all around us. We have not seen the end of abstract art, indeed most likely we have only seen the beginning. Regardless of the possible roles of other styles, it is evident that from the work—and this is far from an exhaustive list—of Arshile Gorky and Jackson Pollock, of Mark Rothko and Clyfford Still, of Willem de Kooning, Jack Tworkov and Franz Kline we are only beginning to learn.

A NOTE ON TERMS AND STYLES

The following brief word list is designed to help the reader who may be puzzled by a given term or who may wish to check on the relevance of a movement or style. It has some of the features of a glossary, providing a brief definition or description where that seems appropriate; and/or giving page references in the text where that seems fitting, it provides an occasional index. The definitions are the author's own and should not be mistaken for representatives of a consensus; like so many, this is a field where a consensus is impossible.

ABSTRACT : There are essentially two kinds of abstraction—one which distills aspects or essences from the object world, and the other which begins with no object at all (for the latter, see *non-objective*). Possible implications of "abstract" and "to abstract" are raised in Chapter VI.

ABSTRACT EXPRESSIONISM : the major painting style of recent years, distilled from abstract art, expressionism and surrealism. See especially pp. 34, 137–60.

ACCIDENT : the exploitation of effects arising from unplanned situations (for example, the dripping of paint). Such practices are traceable at least as far back as Leonardo da Vinci. As with numerous other hallmarks of modern form, the accident has been the victim of recent tendencies to elevate or enlarge certain techniques or approaches into complete schools in themselves.

ACTION PAINTING : sometimes used to describe abstract expressionist styles. Traceable to Jackson's Pollock's "act of painting." See p. 145.

ALL-OVER PAINTING: another concept applied to abstract expressionist styles. As distinguished from the Renaissance tendency toward a single center of tension, all-over painting has multiple centers of tension. Well known to medieval art, it begins to appear again with Monet and with the vanishing of the vanishing point.

ARCHITECTONIC: working with architecture-like structure in painting; to be distinguished from paintings which use architecture-like forms: thus, while Piero della Francesca, Raphael and not infrequently Picasso are architectural painters, Giotto, Cézanne (Color Plate 2) and Braque (Plate 15) are architectonic.

AUTOMATISM: artistic use of impulses, sensations, insights or motifs derived directly from the unconscious. See *Surrealism* especially pp. 121–23.

BAUHAUS: originated in Germany in the 1920's, continued in Chicago in the late thirties, then at Black Mountain and finally at Harvard, Yale and M.I.T. An evangelical school of design, Bauhaus founded architecture-and-art pedagogy upon the intrinsic value of materials and a simplified logic of structure. The ultimate aim was the absorption of all visual arts into a single art of design. It has attracted many architectects and artists, including Walter Gropius, Mies van der Rohe, Josef Albers, Laszlo Moholy-Nagy, Wassily Kandinsky and Paul Klee. While Bauhaus allowed "fine" artists to experiment for experiment's sake, its main goal was to provide a universally recognizable trademark (or concept of design) for a mass audience, as well as to raise the level of modern taste. And while its early products are still highly effective, its overall benefits to the imaginative function in art may be brought into question.

COLLAGE: "pasting" foreign objects or materials (e.g., a piece of bubble gum or a key) onto the canvas. Or a composition made entirely from such materials.

COMPOSE: Used properly, this term—identical with its use in music—is instrumental to an understanding of the creative act in modern art. In the early part of the century a common word for *building a picture* was "construct"; in the twenties this was supplanted by "compose," and in the forties, a favorite verb was "structure." All relate to the same problems (but with slightly varying approaches): resolving the reality of the two-dimensional surface with the illusion of three-dimensional space or the experience of spaciousness, as well as synthesizing compositional elements (shapes and colors, weights and directions) into an organically creative and graspably felt entity. Despite a lot of talk about anti-art, there is no meaningful painting that dispenses with this function.

CRITICISM, ART: a largely spurious activity variously engaged in by poets and professionals, ex-sports writers and aestheticians, pseudonymous authors of mystery stories, and occasionally, in desperation or misguidedness, by artists. Usually eschewed by timorous art historians, it has, however, reached summits at the hands of such older and bolder historians as Julius Meier-Graefe, Kenneth Clark and Lionello Venturi (or more recently, Meyer Schapiro, S. Lane Faison, Jr. and J.P. Hodin), who have not felt superior to the work they dealt with. Art criticism is currently distinguished by a curious self-consciousness and a jerry-built, jangling jargon.

CUBISM: the last significant *aesthetics of the object*. May be distinguished as "analytic" or "synthetic." See Chapter V.

DADA: the first Pop art. Made in Switzerland. Vintage World War I. See pp. 128, 166–67, 172.

DECORATIVE: the most ambivalent art concept of our time. In one sense art is decorative when all aspects find an inseparable expression, as in Michelangelo's Medici Tombs. But the term can also be derogatory, as often in this book, when it refers to work that has "merely" decorative value. Matisse revived the term as one of highest praise to indicate the unity and harmony of a painting with the sense of the wall on which it hangs. It was a daring use and became dangerously confused with "merely decorative," as applied, say, to much late Cubist art. With the return of large-scale painting in Abstract Expressionism, where the painting becomes a kind of wall in itself, the term regains validity. While it is vital—used in this sense—as an approach to

Rothko, Pollock or Kline, it cannot be applied except in the "mere" sense to more superficial contemporaries whose work (like a good deal of Renaissance Mannerist painting), is best seen at a brisk walk through the room in which it hangs, and might therefore be referred to as "Lobby Art." See p. 42.

ENVIRONMENTAL ART: compositions of painting and/or sculpture (possibly including sounds, neon signs or whatever) which provide an environment for the spectator, allowing him to enter physically.

EXPRESSIONISM: Lower-cased, this term refers to broad and recurrent tendencies in Western art, especially in Northern European traditions; capitalized, it refers to specific movements east of the Rhine in the first third of the twentieth century. See pp. 111–20.

FUTURISM: a movement of the early twentieth century which tends to confuse the depiction of action with the action of the picture; its preoccupation with motion is of some interest in relation to Pop and other contemporary modes.

GROUND: the field of the painting, having either a neutral role, as that against which objects are placed, or the positive function (especially since Cézanne) of establishing the dynamics of the surface itself.

HARD-EDGE PAINTING: a newly emergent term with frequent precursors in style; for a good example, note the clarity of shape (the hard, clear edges) in Plate 37. See pp. 178–80.

HUE: technically, refers *only* to the color component (red, yellow, blue and their combinations) in a given tone. See *value*, *intensity* and *tone*; also pp. 27, 54.

IMPRESSIONISM: in lower case refers to various tendencies in painting, from ancient Rome or China to Tiepolo or Turner. Capitalized, it refers to a specific movement, largely French, from the late 1860's to the late 1880's, when it feeds into Post-Impressionism. See pp. 53–60.

INTENSITY: technically, the strength or saturation of a given color independent of its value. See *value;* also p. 54.

KINETIC ART: ordinarily, sculpture with moving parts which operate upon each other or according to some control. A "mobile" is not necessarily kinetic.

MATERIAL: better understood through the French term *matière*. As applied to painting, it has more meanings than any other term I can think of, among the more important: (1) the subject matter of a painting—story, figure, object or expressive theme; (2) the "object" matter—the representation of actual objects; thus Rothko can say quite justly that his painting has subject matter (by having an expressive theme), but no object matter (having no objects represented); (3) represented material—paint which resembles the material of fabrics and jewels, as in the Van Eycks, or flesh and flowers, as in Renoir; (4) paint as a material developed for its own delectation (this, like so much, began with Titian; it is striking in the contemporary work of Rauschenberg or Ossorio); (5) the relationship between (3) and (4) as a vital activity—a major function in Western painting, from Titian to El Greco, Rembrandt to Goya, Courbet to Matisse; (6) a particular sense of weight, texture, density, fluidity, opacity, transparency, coagulation, etc., etc., in the tangible reality (rather than the surface effect) of the paint. See p. 28.

MOTIF: may be used abstractly, as in music, or may be that slice of nature upon which the artist focuses.

NON-OBJECTIVE ART: painting (or sculpture) which does not deal with, or in the strictest sense even refer to, objects. See pp. 28–34, 95, 101.

OP ART: a recent style exploiting or setting forth optical effects as the chief subject of the art; formerly called *trompe-l'œil.* See pp. 173–78.

OPTICAL MIXING: the juxtaposition of pure colors on the canvas, so that the eye itself does the blending—an Impressionist technique, as opposed to the mixing of colors on the palette. See pp. 54–55.

ORGANIC: the most difficult term in contemporary vocabulary and one of the most important. "Organic" means so many things that the reader is best advised to sense the implication from the context. In the broadest sense, all true art is organic—Greek art no less than Gothic (it is *neo*-classical art that is not organic, while Neo-Plasticism, on the other hand, is). A particular concept of the organic as a criterion for modern art can be traced through Louis Sullivan (especially in his *Kindergarten Chats*) to Horatio Greenough (who initiated the notion, so popular in our century, that "form follows function"). As a description of certain qualities commendable in painting, "organic" may suggest a certain tautness (*cf.* the German *Spannung*, as of a violin). The opposite is slackness, whether of the relation of subject to form, or in the form itself. (This sort of slackness abounds in the later work of Picasso or Larry Rivers.) Among many other connotations is that of natural growth, as in an artist's career: thus the careers of Cézanne, Monet, Mondrian and De Kooning are highly organic, whereas Picasso's brilliant career, unexampled in its range, appears more as a kaleidoscope of stylistic changes, each seeking to outdistance his own protean performances.

PASSAGE: in painting as in music and in literature.

PLASTIC: a term given ethical as well as aesthetic value by both Mondrian and Hofmann, possibly to rescue painting from literary surrealism. "Plastic" emphasizes the integrity of the two-dimensional quality of the canvas, the balance of negative and positive space, the balance of color in the composition, the integration of subject and object matter. When all functions are balanced and all elements integrated—as in Giotto, Cézanne, Mondrian or Matisse—a picture may be called plastic. Dali is not plastic.

POP ART: short for "popular," as in "pop" music. A revivalist term. Pop artists have, however, nothing in common with the "popular masters" of the twenties, such as Vivin, Seraphine or John Kane. See pp. 166–73.

POST-IMPRESSIONISM: a variety of synthesizing styles dominating the last fifteen years of the nineteenth century, and featuring Cézanne, Van Gogh, Seurat, Gauguin. It absorbed Impressionism, often giving it symbolic overtones. See pp. 58–77.

PRIMITIVE: a symptom of twentieth-century yearning for purity and lost innocence. It may include "true" primitive (Easter Islands); the sophisticated primitive (Benin bronzes); the backwoods of a civilization (seventeenth-century Brittany or eighteenth-century America); the civilized ingénu (Douanier Rosseau, Art Brut and Dubuffet); the early form of a high civilization (Celtic manuscripts, early Romanesque sculpture) or even of a developed movement (though fortunately people no longer speak of Italian fourteenth-century painting as "primitive"); or the more or less conscious and certainly sophisticated absorption of ancient or exotic forms into twentieth-century painting and sculpture. This includes not merely the obvious influence of African tribal art on Modigliani or Picasso, but the perhaps still more essential if less recognized debt of some of Picasso's "pure" inventions to Mycenaean art, or of Brancusi's "pure" sculpture to Cycladic forms.

SPECTRAL PALETTE: using only the colors of sunlight (as discernable through a prism or in a rainbow). See pp. 54–55.

SUPREMATISM: a term coined by Malevich to express the ultimate in non-objective art. See p. 109.

SURREALISM: originally a literary movement that incorporated Dadaism, directed from its inception by André Breton. It emphasized the unconscious as a source of inspiration and was opposed to constructed and figuratively inspired art. It influenced Miró and Picasso in his *Guernica* period, passing thus to Pollock and Motherwell. Surrealism espoused every unconscious process—e.g., automatism, automatic writing, disassociation and juxtaposition of symbols, dreams, sex imagery. In a further effort to awaken the total artist, it espoused radical politics and the life of action. Its influence continues in contemporary cinema, Pop art, Beat literature, happenings, typography, etc. See pp. 120–26.

TONE: technically, a given condition of hue, value and intensity of paint under a given light at a given distance.

VALUE: the lightness or darkness of a tone without regard to hue or intensity. See pp. 27, 54.

WASH: a technique developed in ink drawing and water color (the wash drawings of Rembrandt, Goya, Constable, the water colors of Turner); extended in recent years to oil painting on unsized canvas, with a resulting spontaneity and brilliance of surface. It is another valid painting technique that has been appropriated as a gimmick defining a school.

ABOUT THE AUTHOR

John P. Sedgwick, Jr., born in Cambridge, Massachusetts, in 1925, graduated from Williams College in 1947 and was awarded a Ph.D. in art history by Harvard in 1954. He has taught at Columbia University and Hunter College, and is now Professor of Art in the University of North Carolina at Greensboro. In 1951–52 he studied in Paris on a Fulbright grant, and in 1953 received a Ford grant.

An artist himself, Mr. Sedgwick has had two one-man shows of his drawings at a New York gallery. He has written articles for *Art News* and the *Encyclopedia Americana*, and is the author of *Art Appreciation Made Simple, Structure and Evolution of the Major Cultures*, and *Highlights: An Illustrated History of Art*, with E. M. Upjohn.